TEXTURES

First published 1990 by
éditions Aubrey Walter/GMP Publishers Ltd
P O Box 247, London N17 9QR
Telephone 081-365 1545 Fax 081-365 1252

Designed and packaged by GMP Publishers Ltd.

British Library in Cataloguing in Publication Data
Truitt, Warren
Textures : photos.
1. American photographs. Special subjects: Men: Nudes
I. Title II. Lucie–Smith, Edward, 1933–
779.23092

ISBN 0–85449 –128–7

Distributed in North America by Alyson Publications Inc.,
40 Plympton Street, Boston, Ma 02118, USA.

Distributed in Australia by Stilone Pty Ltd.,
P O Box 155, Broadway, NSW 2007, Australia.

Printed and reproduced in Hong Kong
by South Sea International Press Ltd.

TEXTURES

photographs by
WARREN TRUITT

introduced by
EDWARD LUCIE-SMITH

GMP
éditions
Aubrey Walter

warren truitt

In the past, the male nude was one of the great forbidden subjects in photography — which is not the same thing as saying that photographers didn't attempt it. Almost from the very beginning, photographs were made of naked men. At first these studies were said to be "scientific" — and scientific purpose was genuinely present in the motion studies of Eadweard Muybridge and Etienne J Marey. Such images were also said to be "artistic" — Delacroix had photographs of nude models, male and female, produced for his own use; and photographs of male nudes were made by commercial photographers "for the use of artists". Clearly, however, some of these were bought and kept for other reasons. Von Gloeden was perhaps the first photographer to make photographs of male nudes which were intended to be independent art objects. He succeeded in producing homoerotic versions of Alma–Tadema. He was followed by turn of the century Pictorialist photographers such as F Holland Day, and from these there descends a long tradition of distinguished photographers who have made male nudes at least part of their characteristic subject matter. The names that come to mind include those of George Platt Lynes, Robert Mapplethorpe, George Dureau and Bruce Weber.

It is perhaps no accident that so many of the leading photographers of the male nude, in the course of the last 80 years, should have been American. The relationship between photography and more traditional kinds of image–making — painting and drawing — is subtly different historically in the United States from the situation prevailing in Europe. Painting, as a means of artistic expression, is less deeply rooted in American culture: the pioneers relied on the camera, rather more than the brush, to bring them images of the new lands they were making their own. The photographic work done by the Precisionists — some of whom, like Charles Sheeler, were accomplished photographers — and still more so the close personal and artistic relationship between the photographer Stieglitz and the painter Georgia O'Keefe, pulled photography towards the centre, and helped to establish its status as a major vehicle of artistic creativity. Since World War II, Pop artists like Andy Warhol, and Super Realists like Chuck Close, have helped to break down any remaining barriers between the aesthetics of photography and those of painting. During the past decade, the increasingly esoteric nature of New York School painting — its tendency to hold a private introverted dialogue with the theoreticians of Modernism such as Marcel Duchamp — has tended to further exalt the position of the artist whose instrument is the camera. Robert Mapplethorpe's rapid and overwhelming success in the late 1970s and the 1980s owed something to the supposedly "scandalous" nature of some of his subject matter. Paradoxically, it owed quite as much to the fact that his supremely elegant and disciplined images — his characteristic flowers as well as his characteristic nudes — were accessible to a much wider audience than anything produced by the painters who were his rivals within the New York art arena.

The photography of the male nude benefits from the centrality accorded to photography in general within the American tradition. It also has a special edge, due to the patterns of American society. If one looks at America, from a vantage point in Europe, this society often seems to be a bizarre, dissonant mixture of the libertarian and the puritanical. There is great emphasis on personal liberty, including liberty of sexual choice. There is also a strong, but uneven emphasis, on "traditional" moral standards, by which is largely meant the standards and values of 19th century Protestantism. The struggle between these attitudes reaches occasional moments of direct confrontation — a recent example was the cancellation of a Mapplethorpe retrospective at the Corcoran Art Gallery in Washington after protests, and threats to funding, made by conservative members of Congress.

The situation affects the American photographer who is interested in the male nude in several ways. He runs a constant risk of "ghettoisation". That is, he can make photographs which are quite openly and blatantly erotic, so long as there is an implicit acknowledgement — both by means of the actual type of image chosen, and its context (its presentation in a gay magazine, for example, surrounded by erotic fiction), that he is prepared to confine his audience to a minority — an audience of homosexual men, happy to acknowledge their own homosexuality. If the photographer does not want to take this route, he has to accept the fact that there will be a constant tension in his relationship with his audience. Is this art — or is it sex ? And what happens when the answer is both.

Warren Truitt makes it clear that the second route — the rejection of the ghetto — is the one which he has decided to take. These are studies of males — naked males, often with an emphasis on sexuality. They are also carefully considered classical compositions, in which everything visible counts — not merely the actual body depicted, with all the particularity which only the camera can give, but its relationship to its surroundings, and the pattern of light and shade, solid and void made by the whole image.

The fact that all the models are anonymous, in the precise sense that the photographs crop or conceal heads, or show them only from angles where the face is concealed, stresses the point that the male nude, here, is treated as raw material. It is shaped and edited so as to convey a particular vision of the subject. This vision, however, does not omit sexuality. In fact, very much the contrary. It often concentrates on details, such as the presence of veins under the skin, the texture of skin itself, and the pattern and texture of body hair, which are precisely those which most of us tend to focus upon at moments of heightened eroticism. In fact, the particular character of the photographs comes from the extremely cool, rational nature of the approach to problems of composition, and the hypersensibility found in the approach to details. This combination is the reason why Warren Truitt has something valuable to add to the already long and fascinating history of the depiction of the male nude in American photography.

Edward Lucie–Smith
London 1990

photographer's note

The pictures in this collection were all made in the area of Tucson, Arizona between 1982 and 1989. Models are identified by first names only, and no faces are ever shown so that the viewer will be more objective in assessing the unique beauty of a natural male body. All the models are non-professional and were given minimal direction. Few had ever posed nude before though some were drafted from life-drawing classes or referred by other artists. Their ages range from nineteen to forty-five years. With a few exceptions, they are sequenced in related pairs: from standing poses through sitting or crouching to reclining.

All of the negatives were exposed with a Yashica twin-lens reflex camera on Ilford 120 film, using ASA 50; the full frame was almost never used, refining of the compostion being done in the darkroom.

I entered photography from the world of the visual arts. I am a professional artist in the media of painting, collage and poetry. I have also worked for 35 years or so in commercial design. Though I have studied and appreciated the work of other photographers such as von Gloeden, Platt Lynes, Dureau and Mapplethorpe the single most important influence on my work has been that of Minor White. It is the mystical quality of his work, his materializing of light and his exquisite compositioins that attract me. If I have a distinct style, it is 'designing with the male figure'.

Warren Truitt
Tucson, Arizona 1989

To Ron, without whom this would never have been.
And a special thanks to
Dan, Bob, and Keith for your continued encouragement
and always constructive criticism.

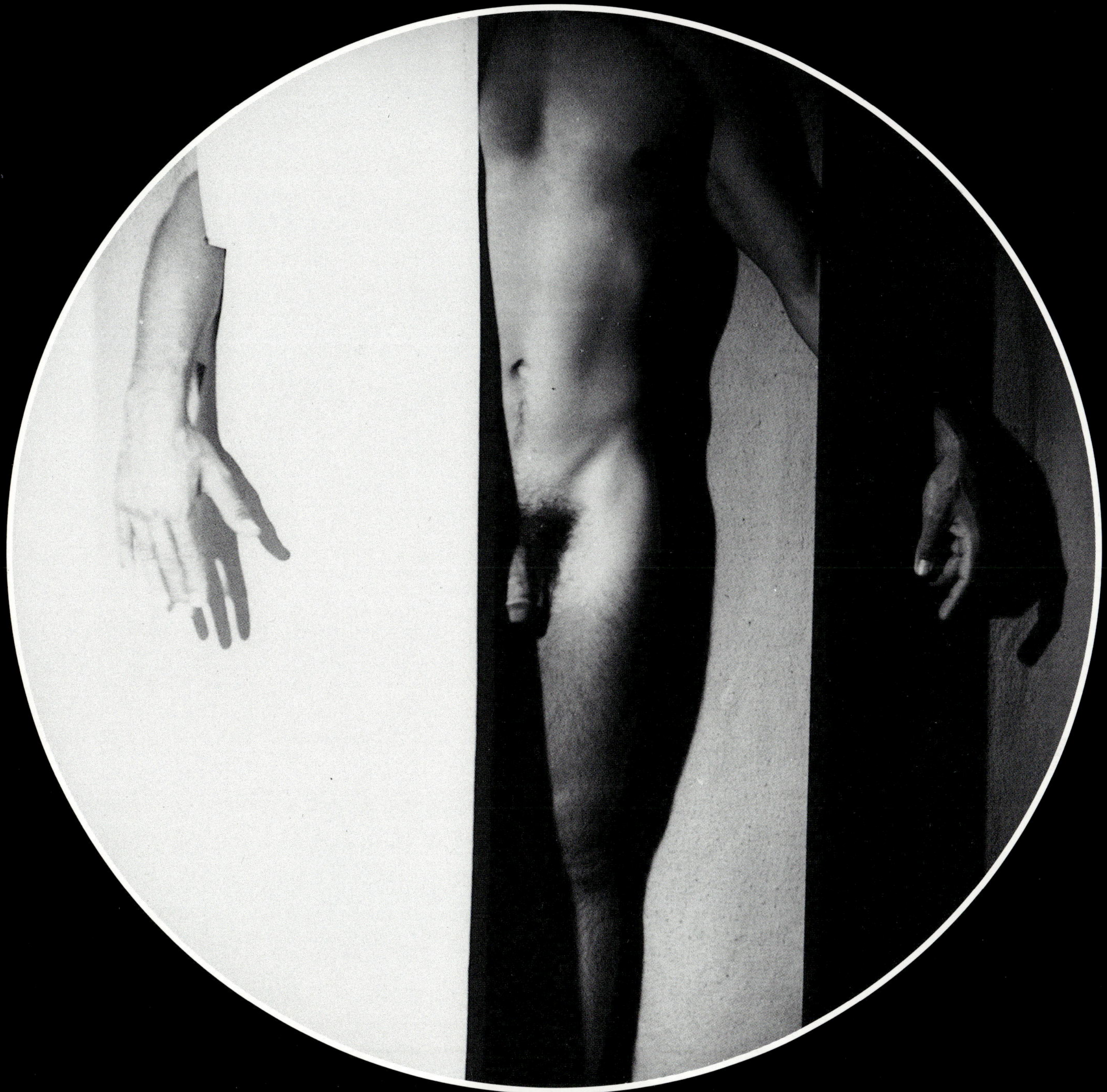

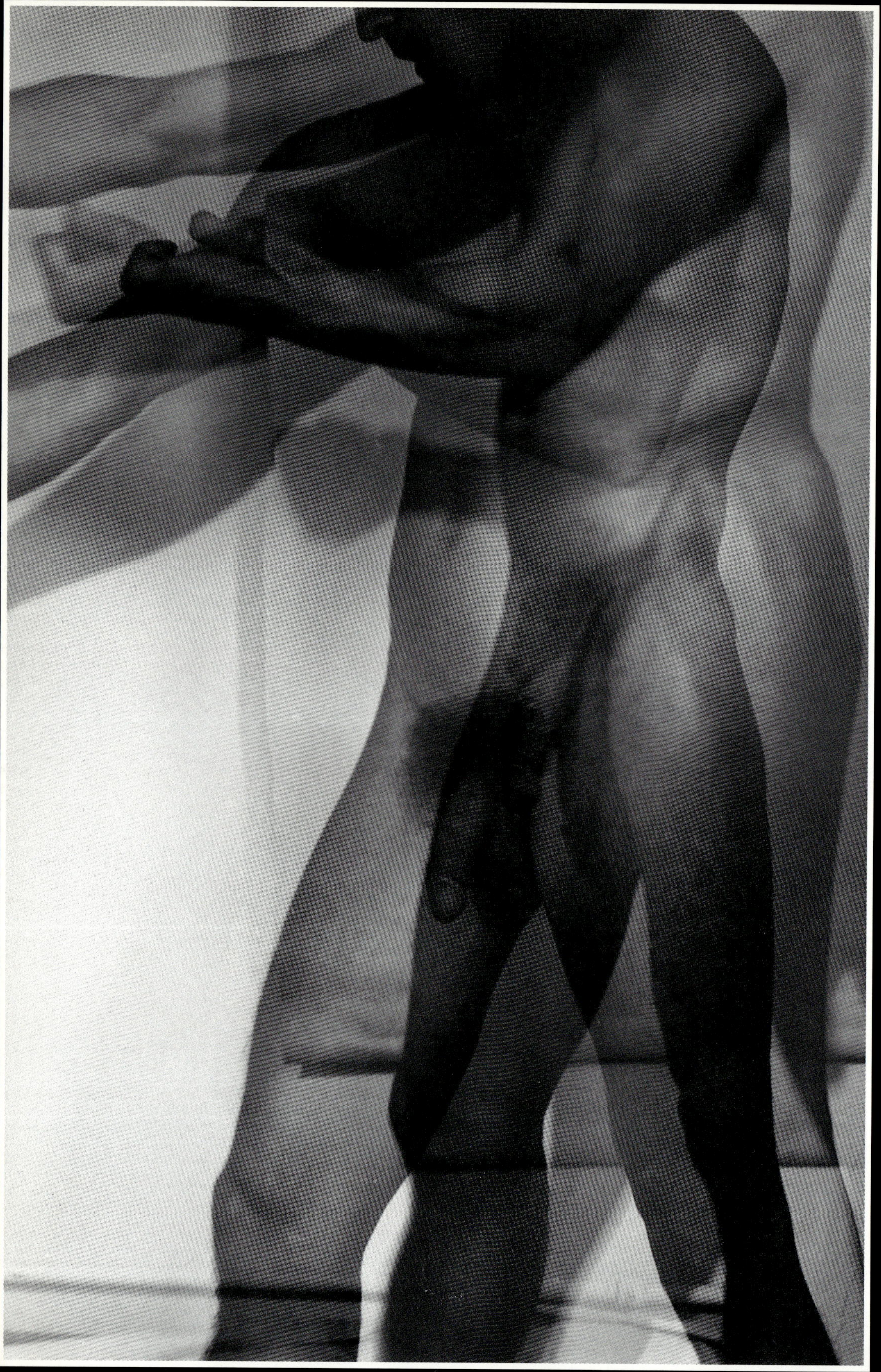

Chris

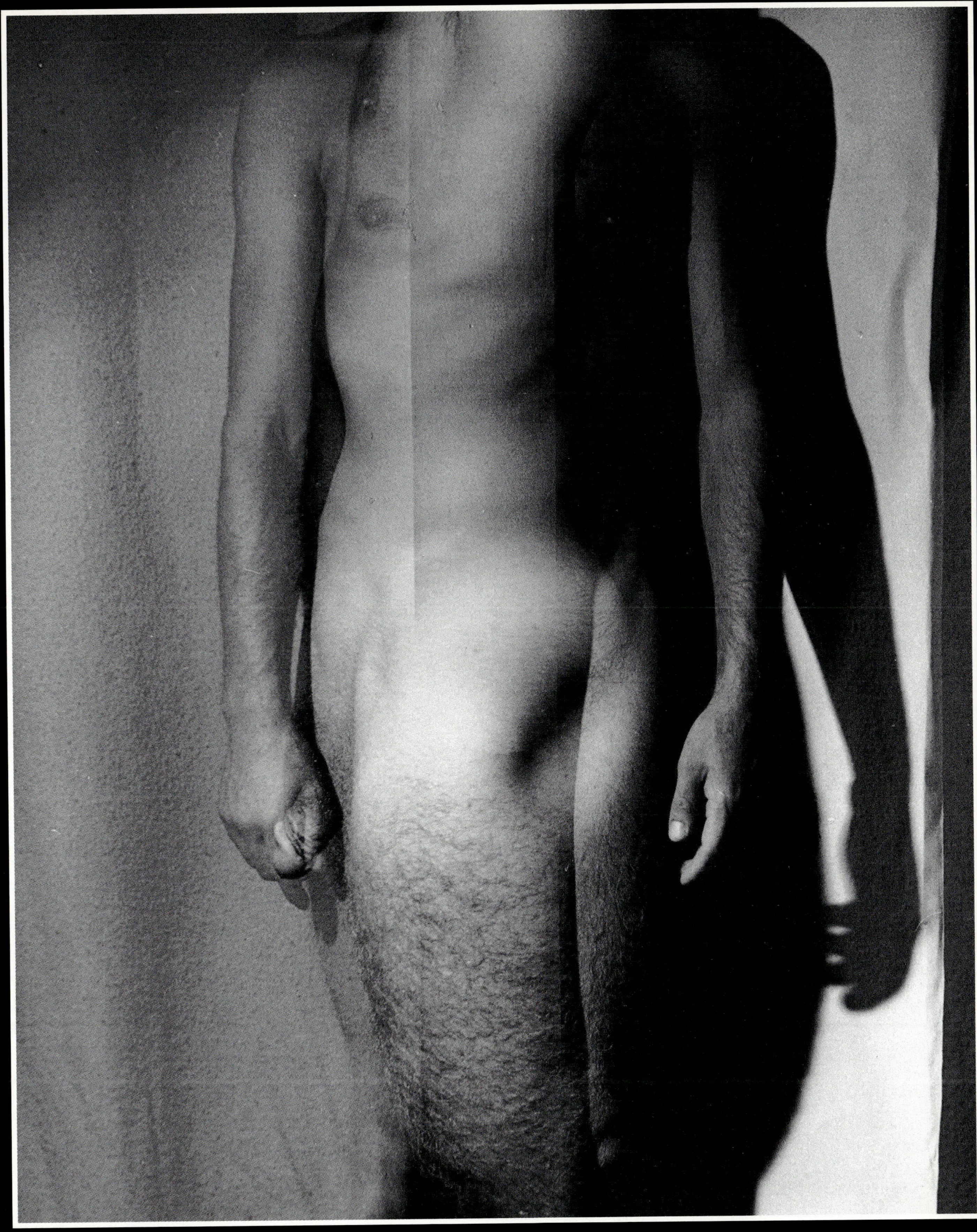

Michael S

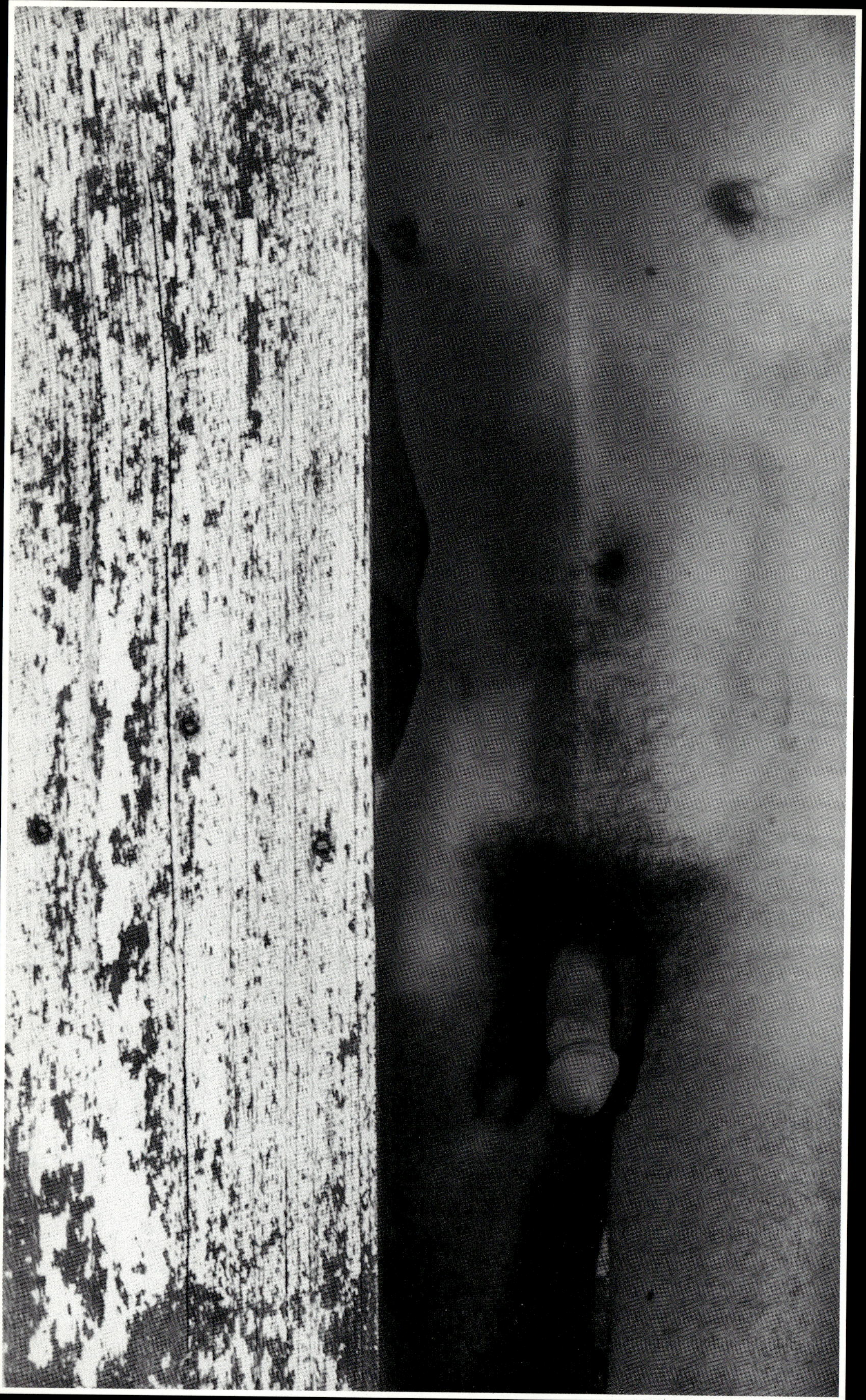

 Tom Wl

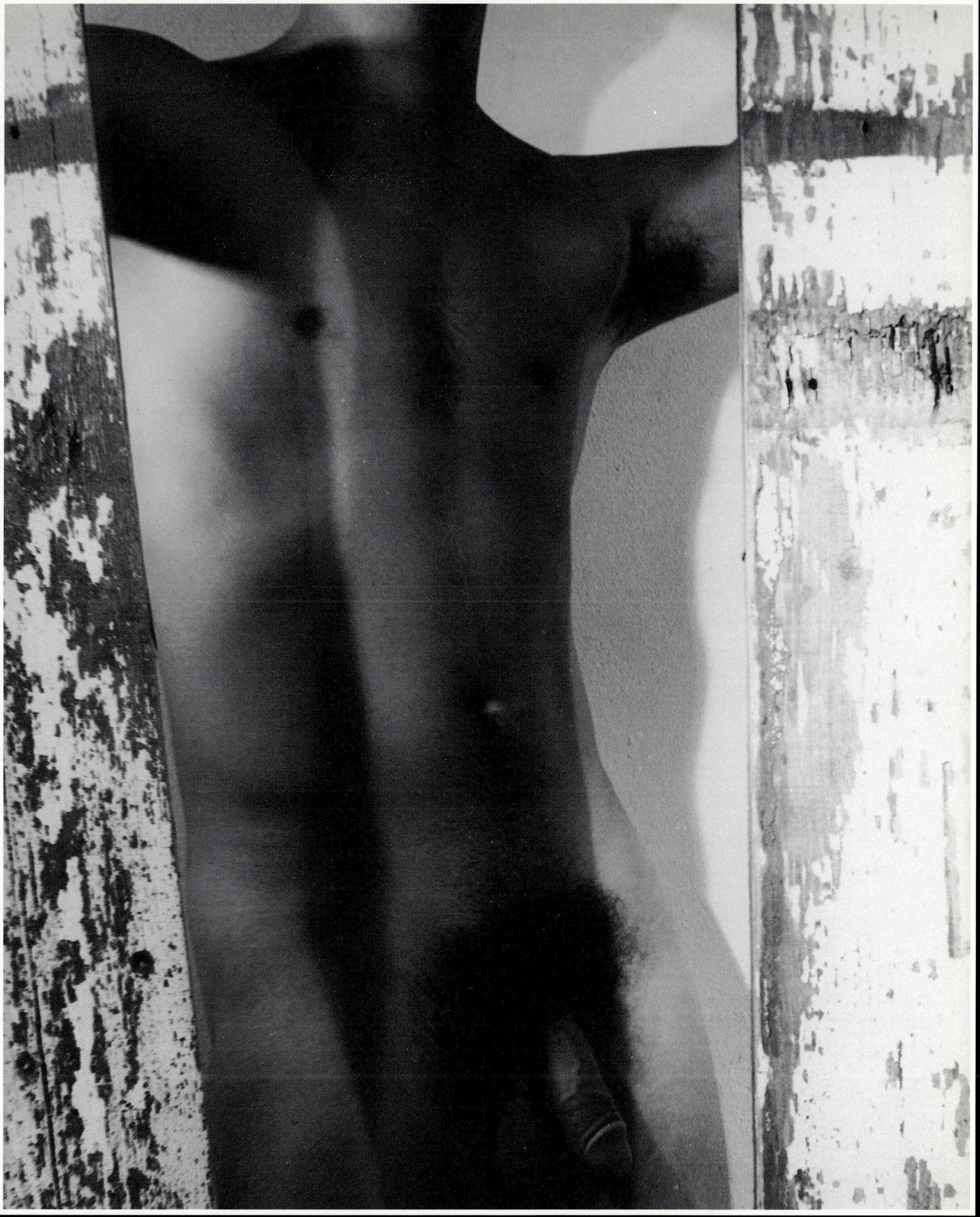

John

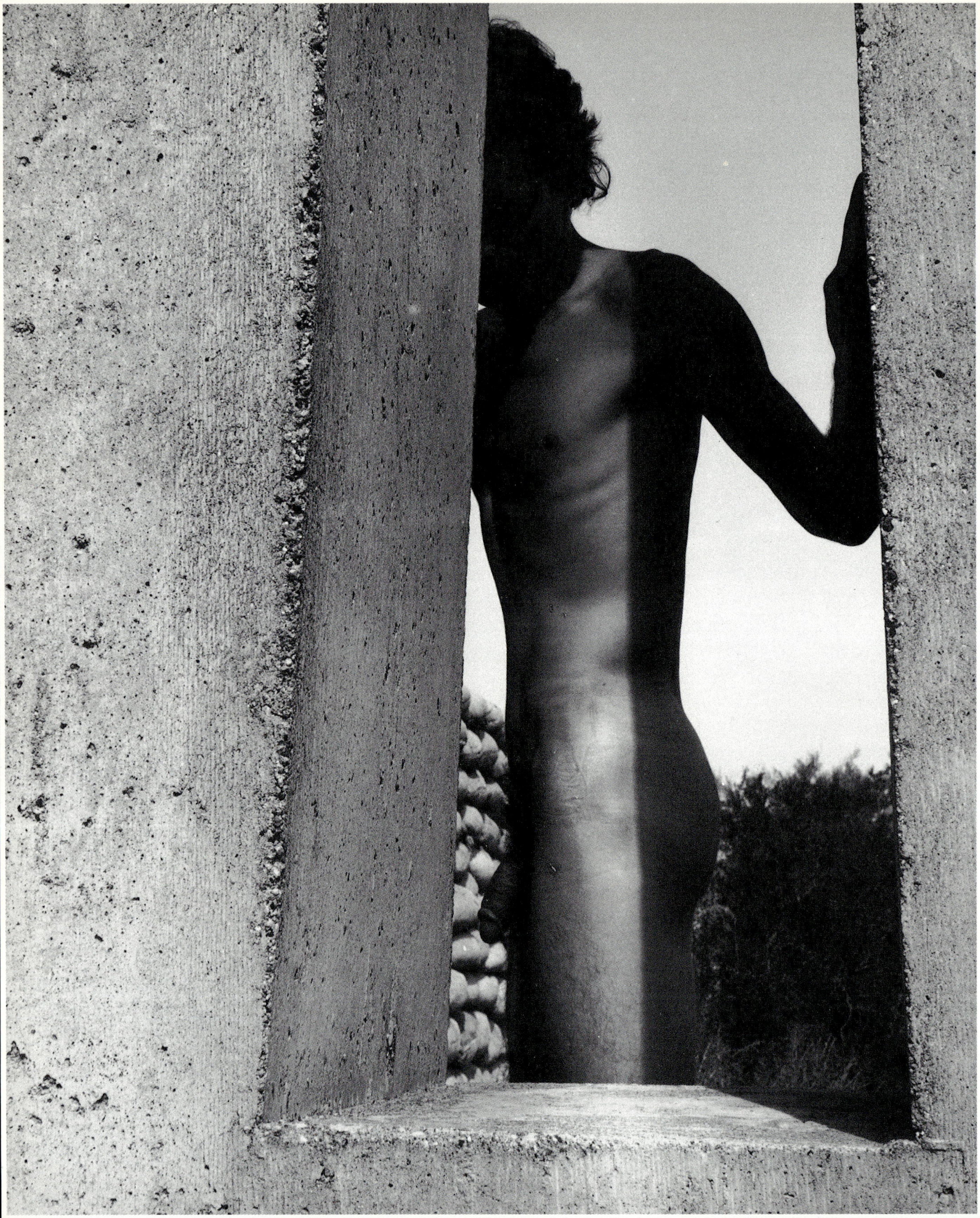

Jimm'z

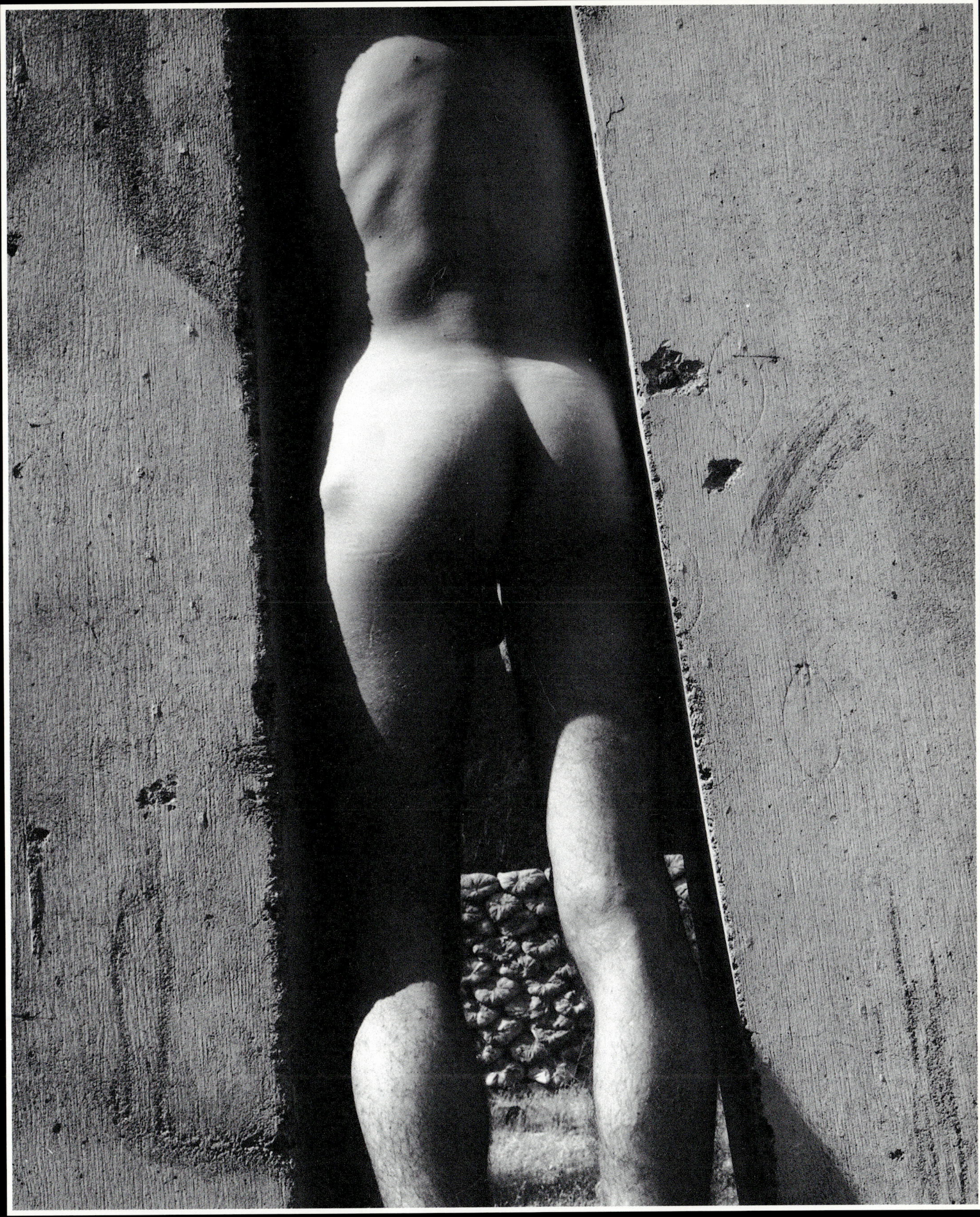

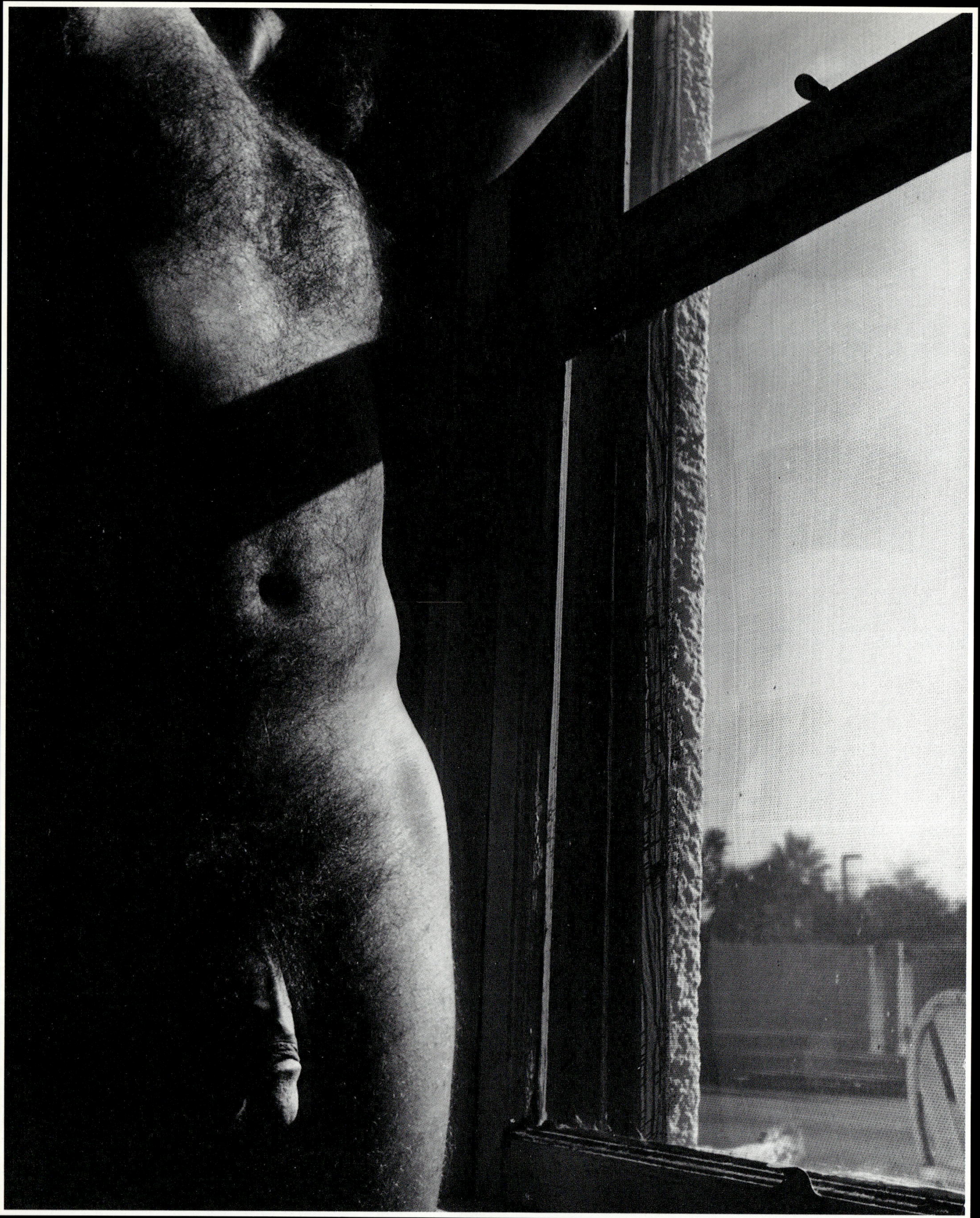

George

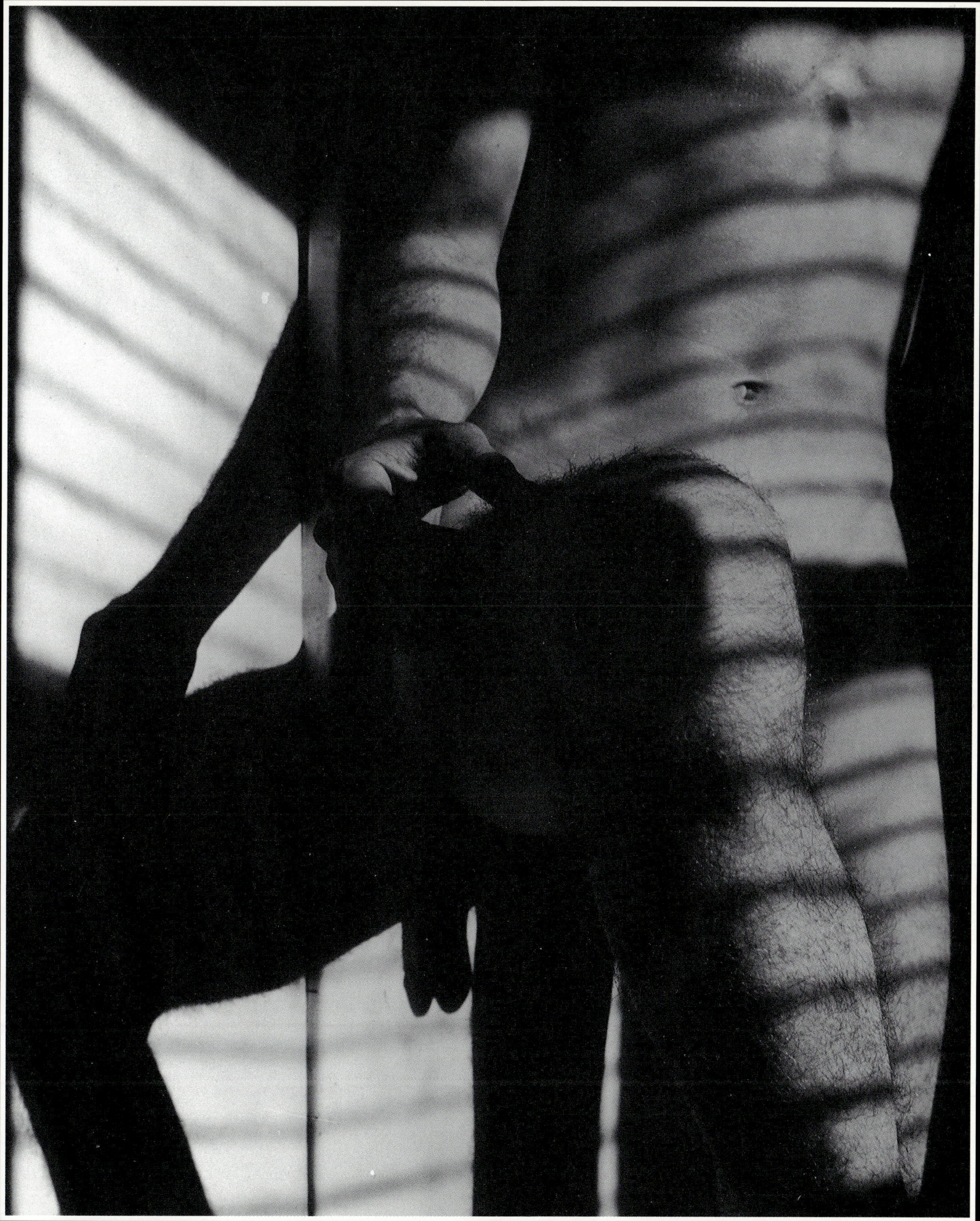

John

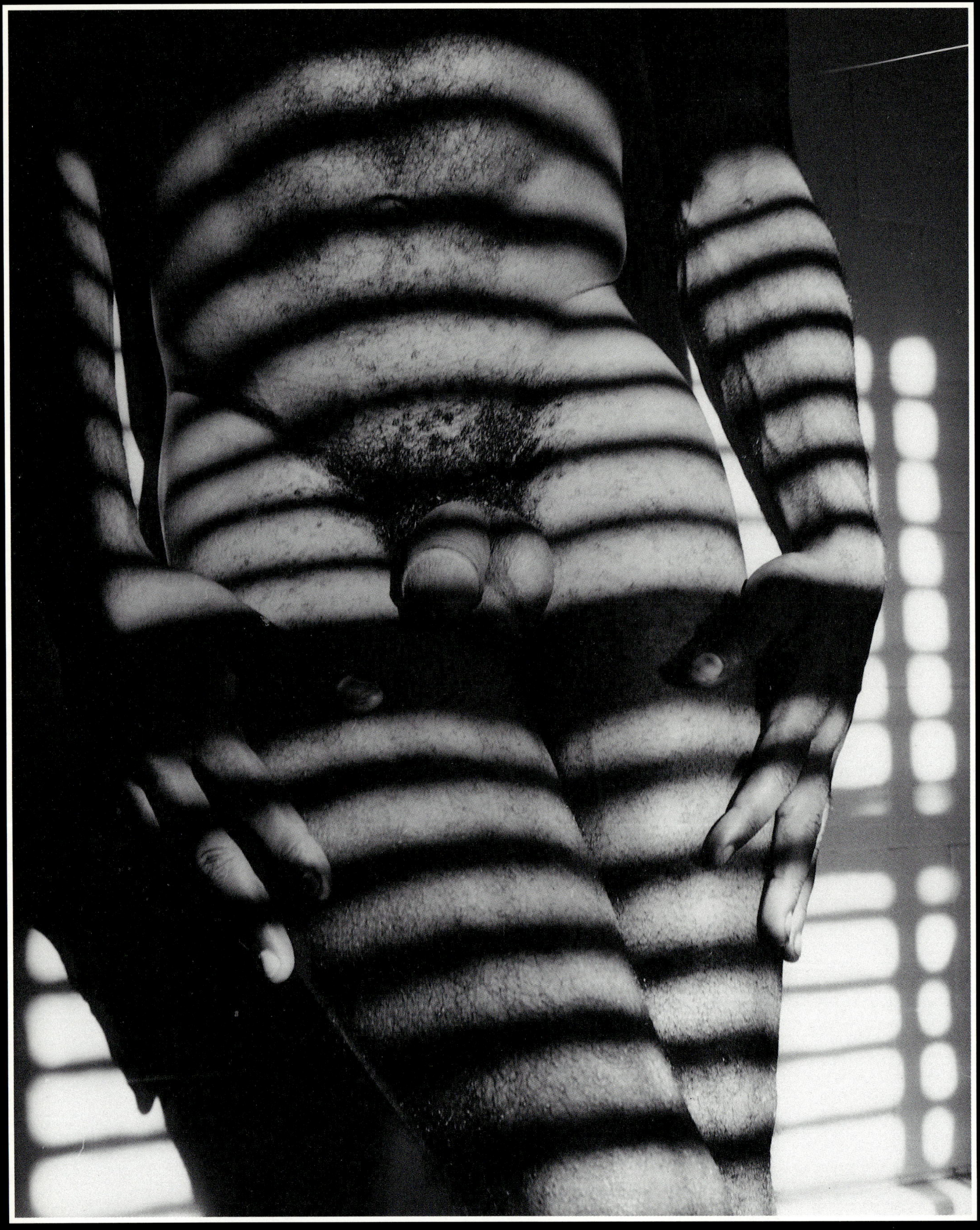

Robbin

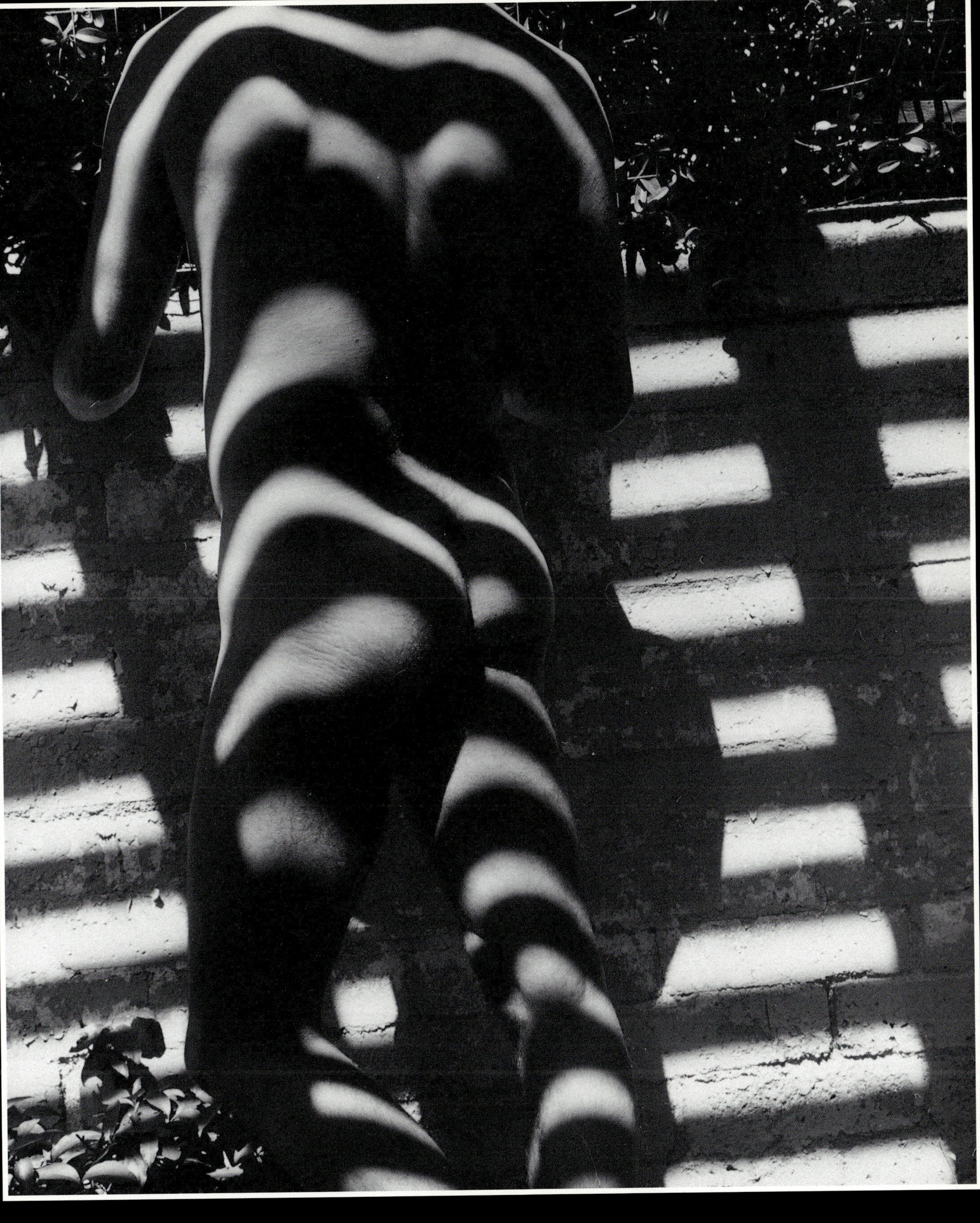

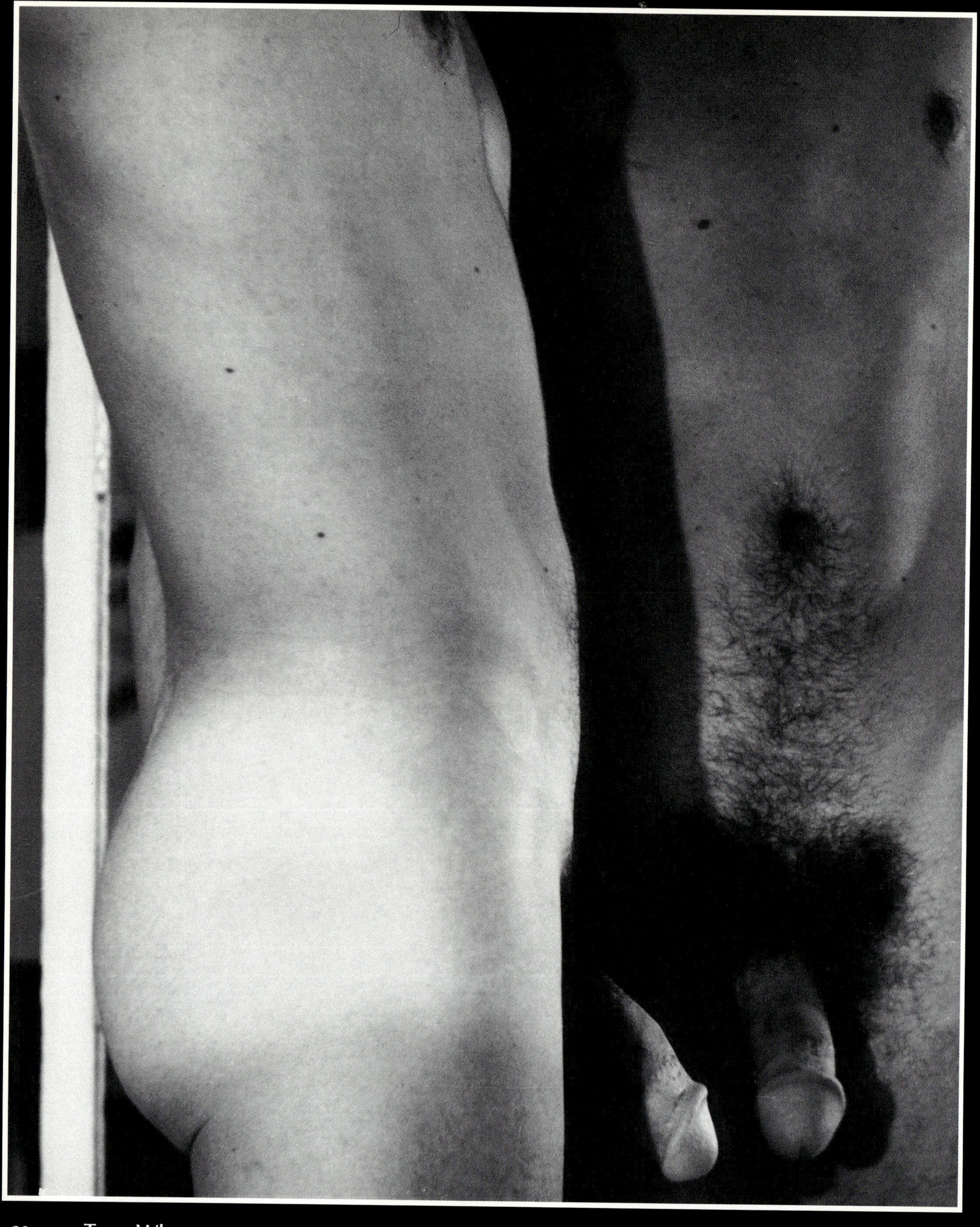

 Tom WI

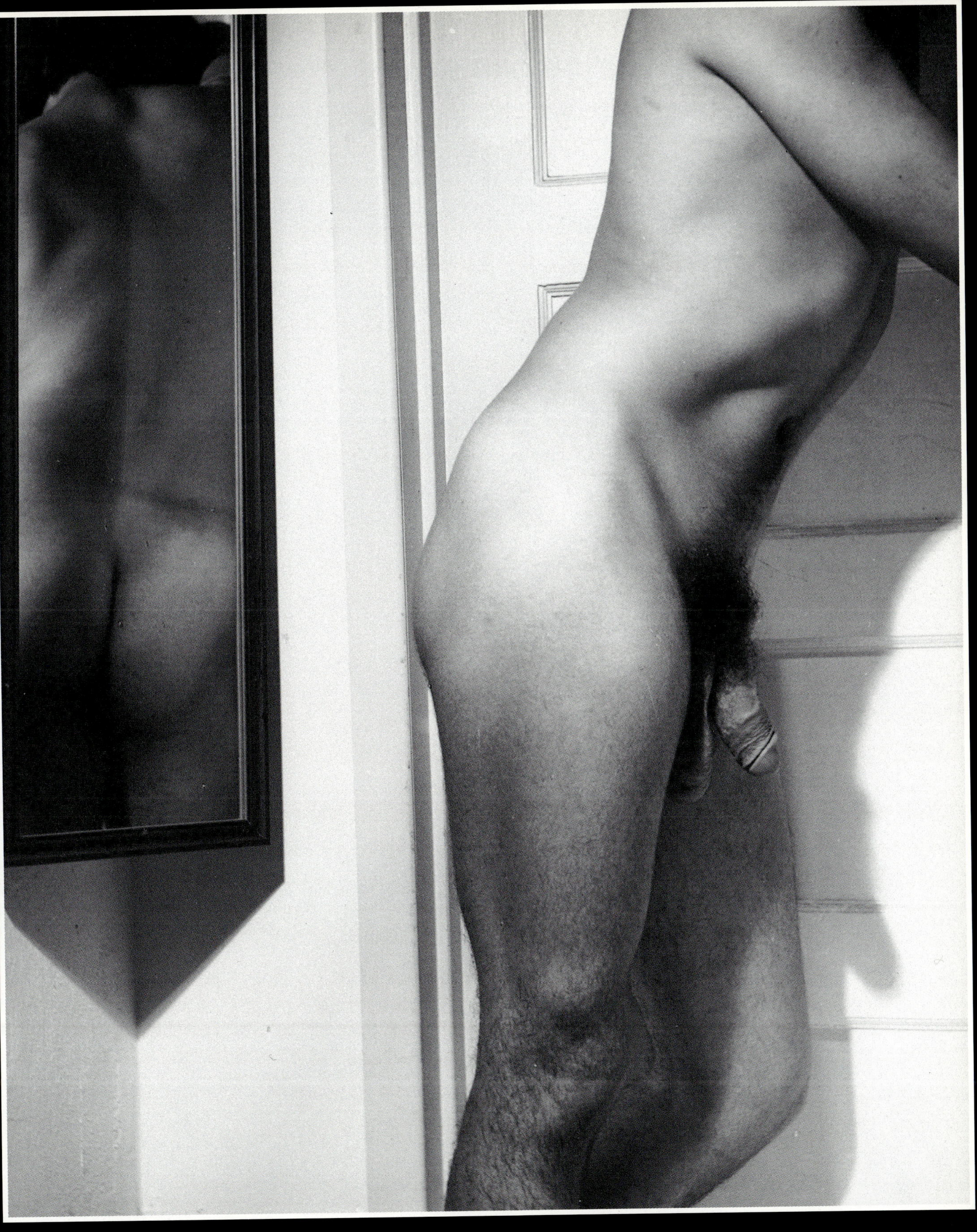

John

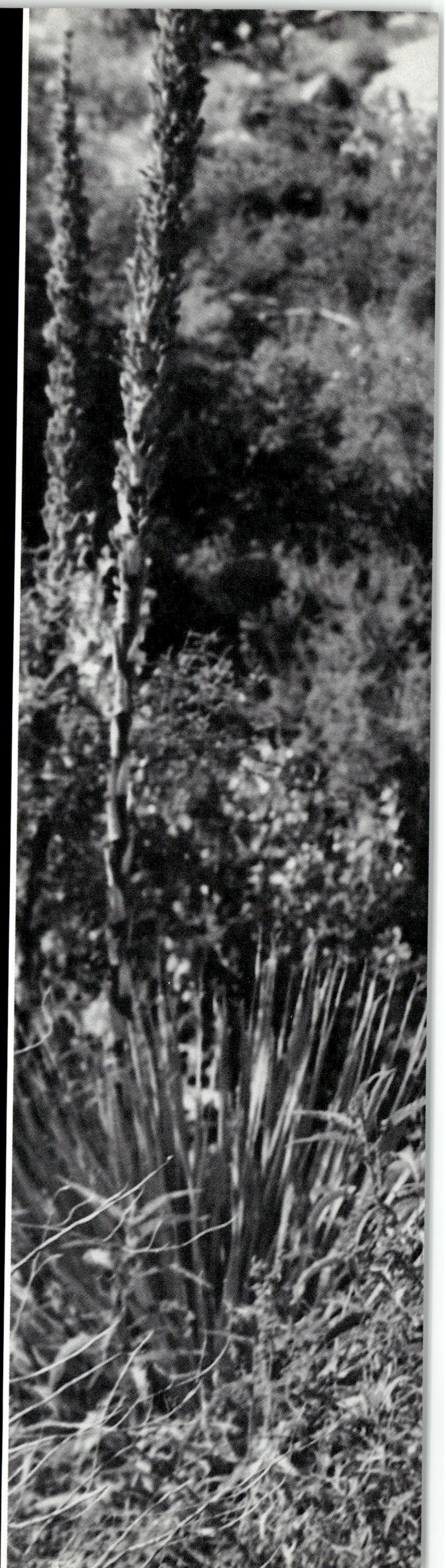

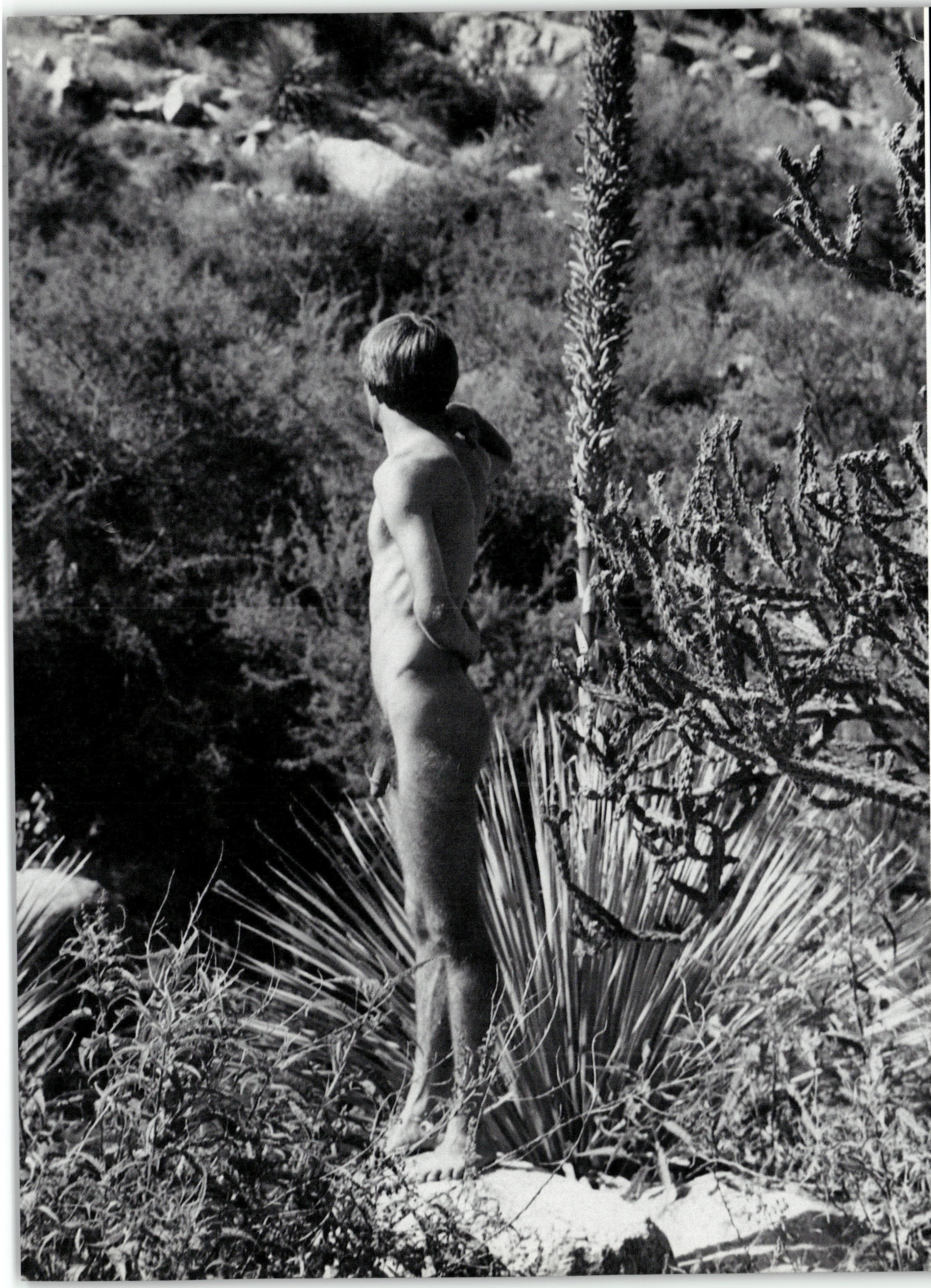

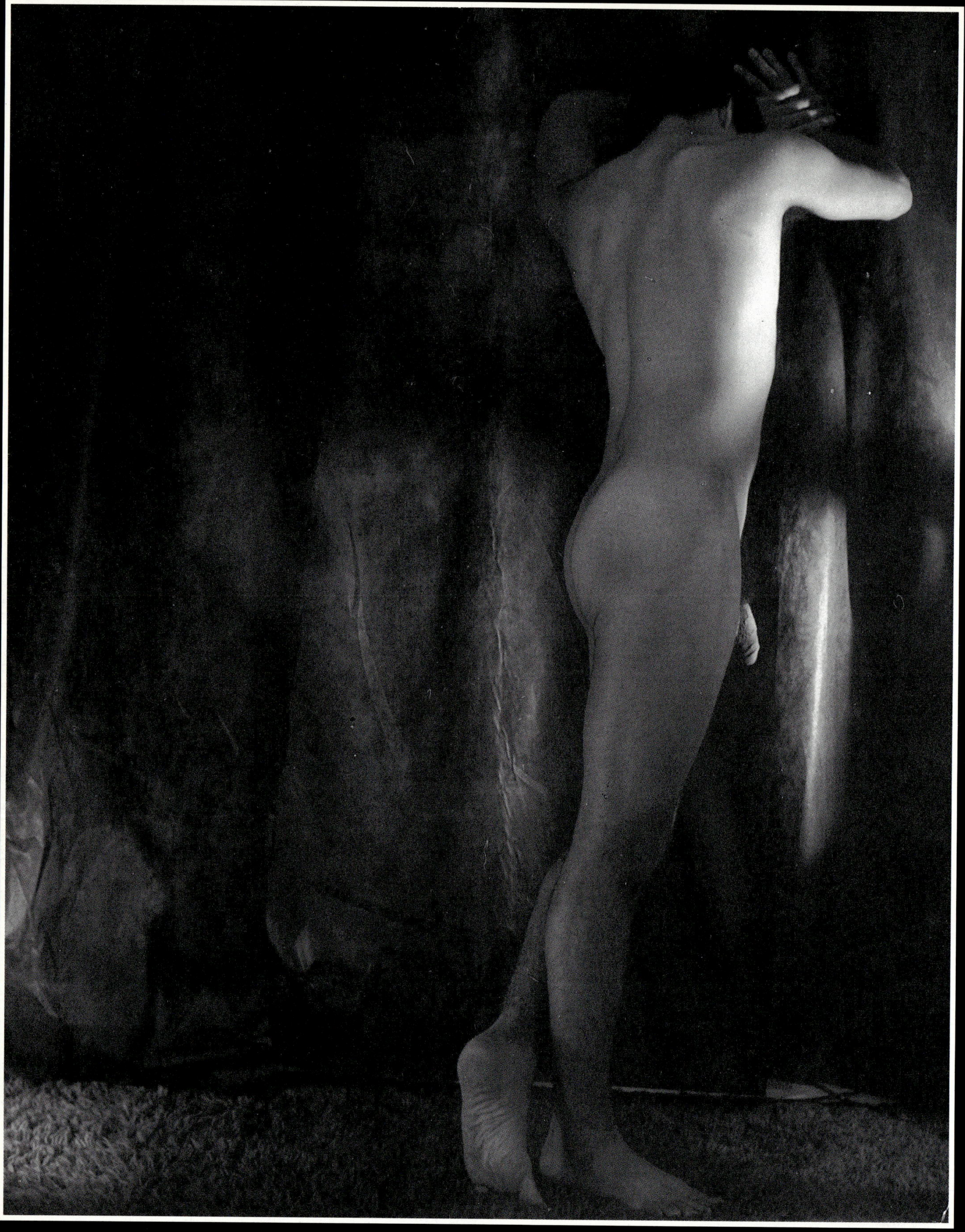

 John

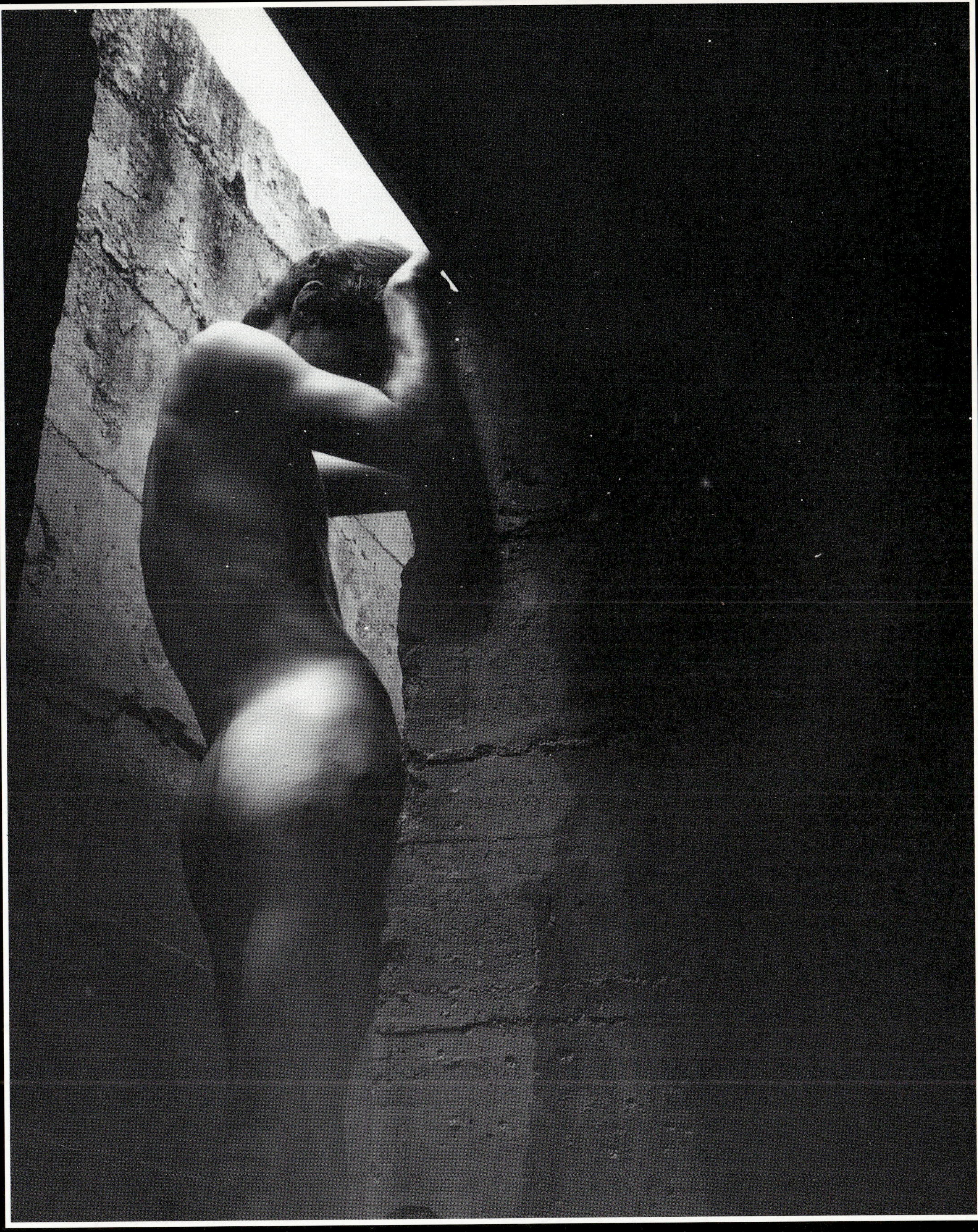

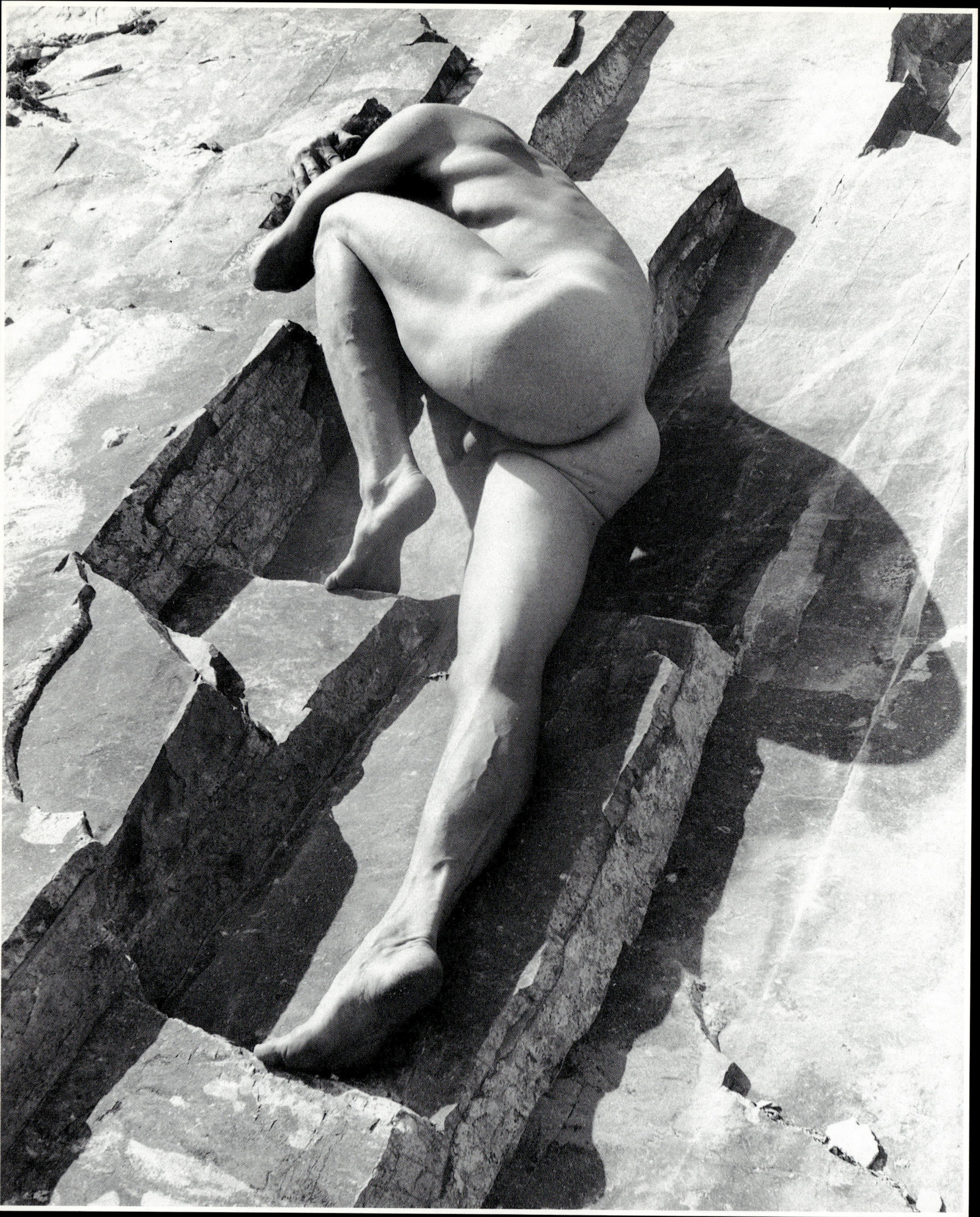

Greg

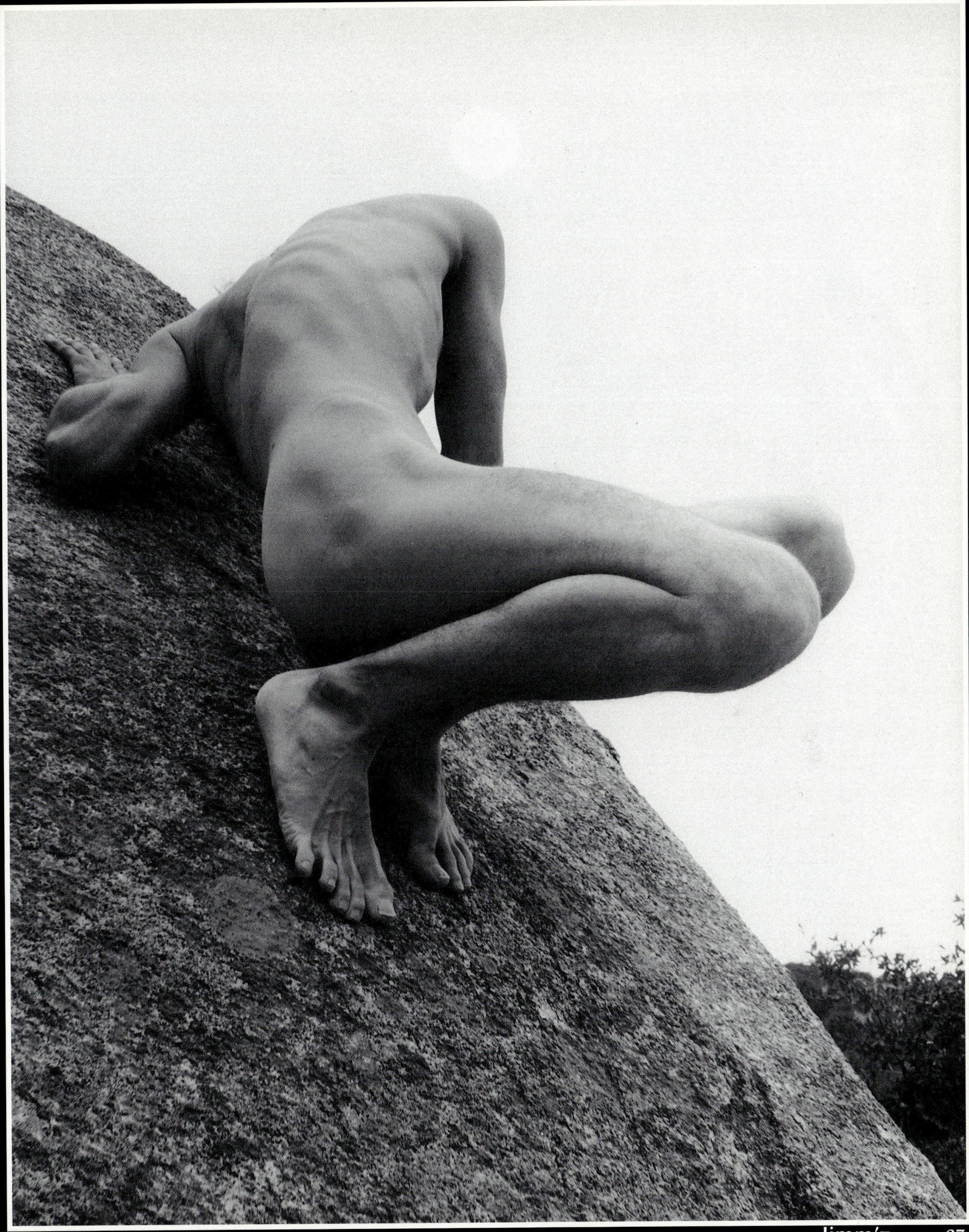

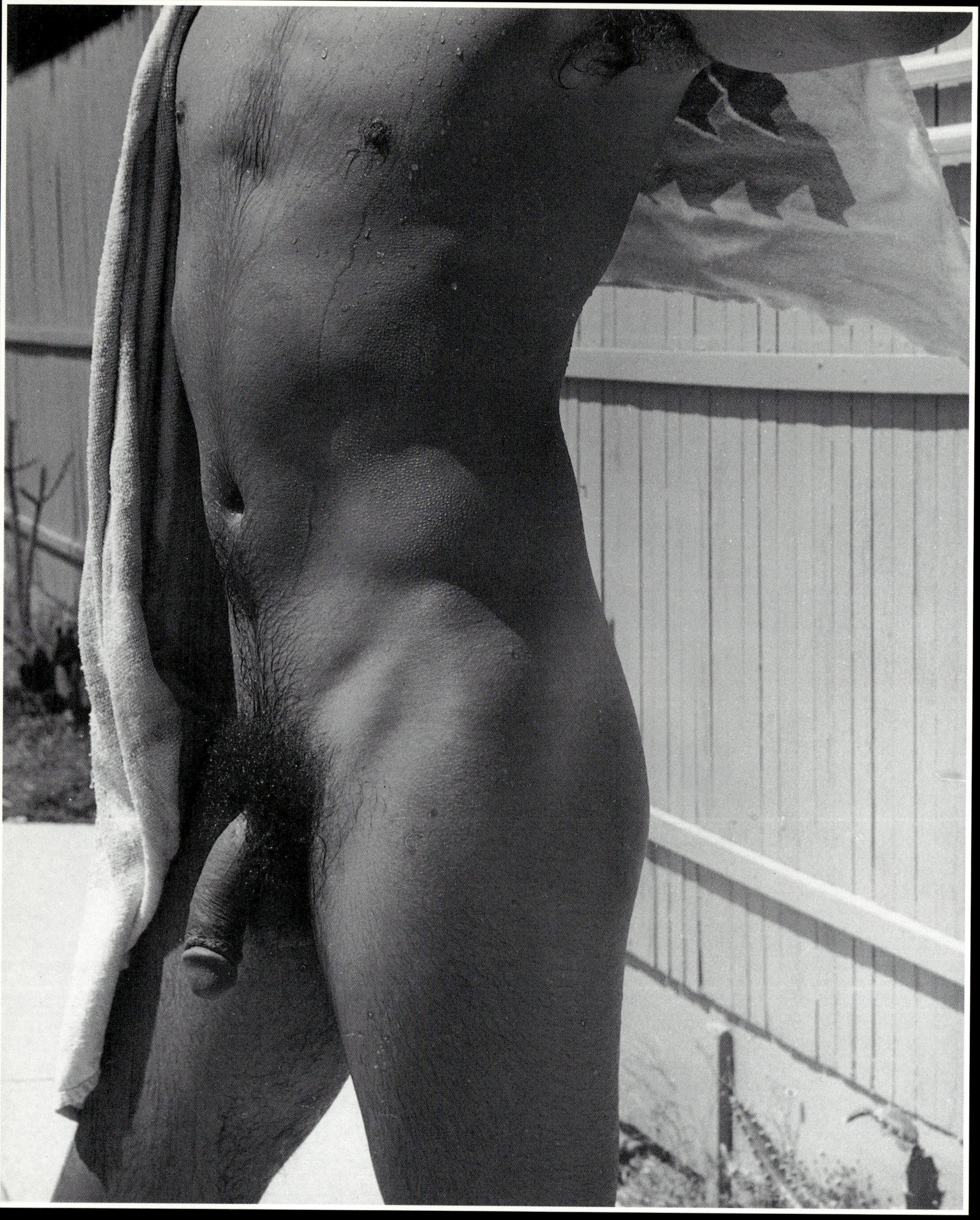

 John

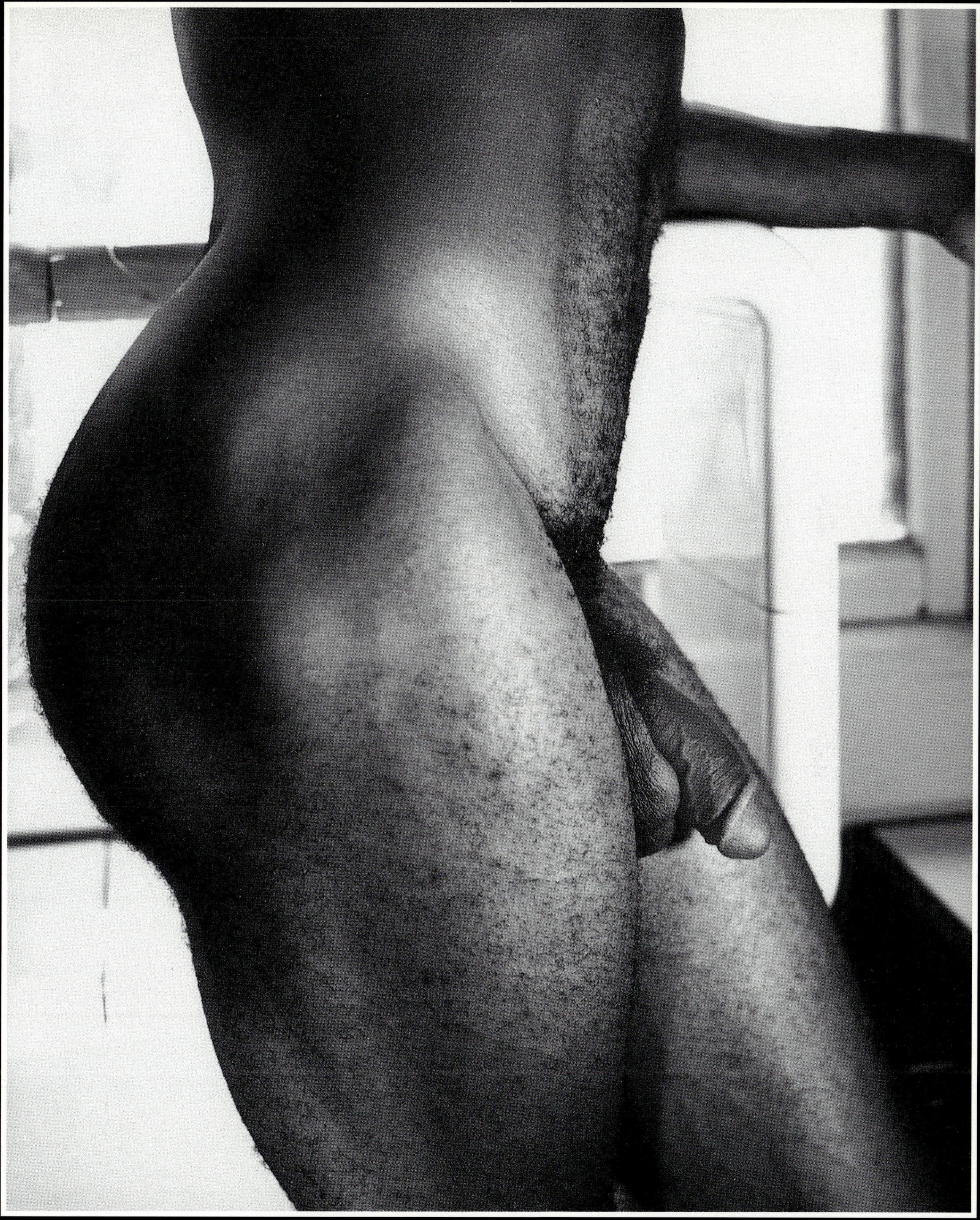

Robbin

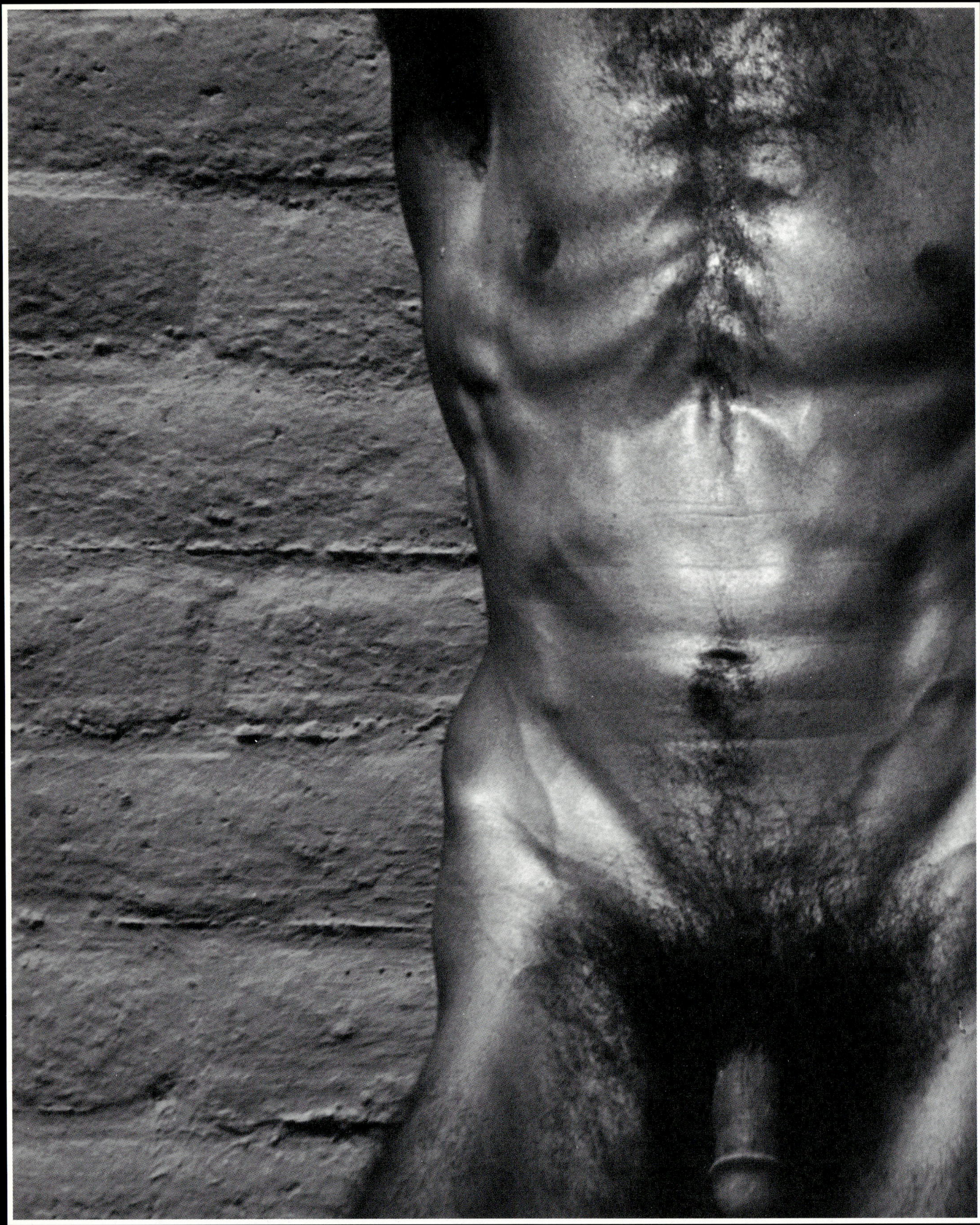

Wayne

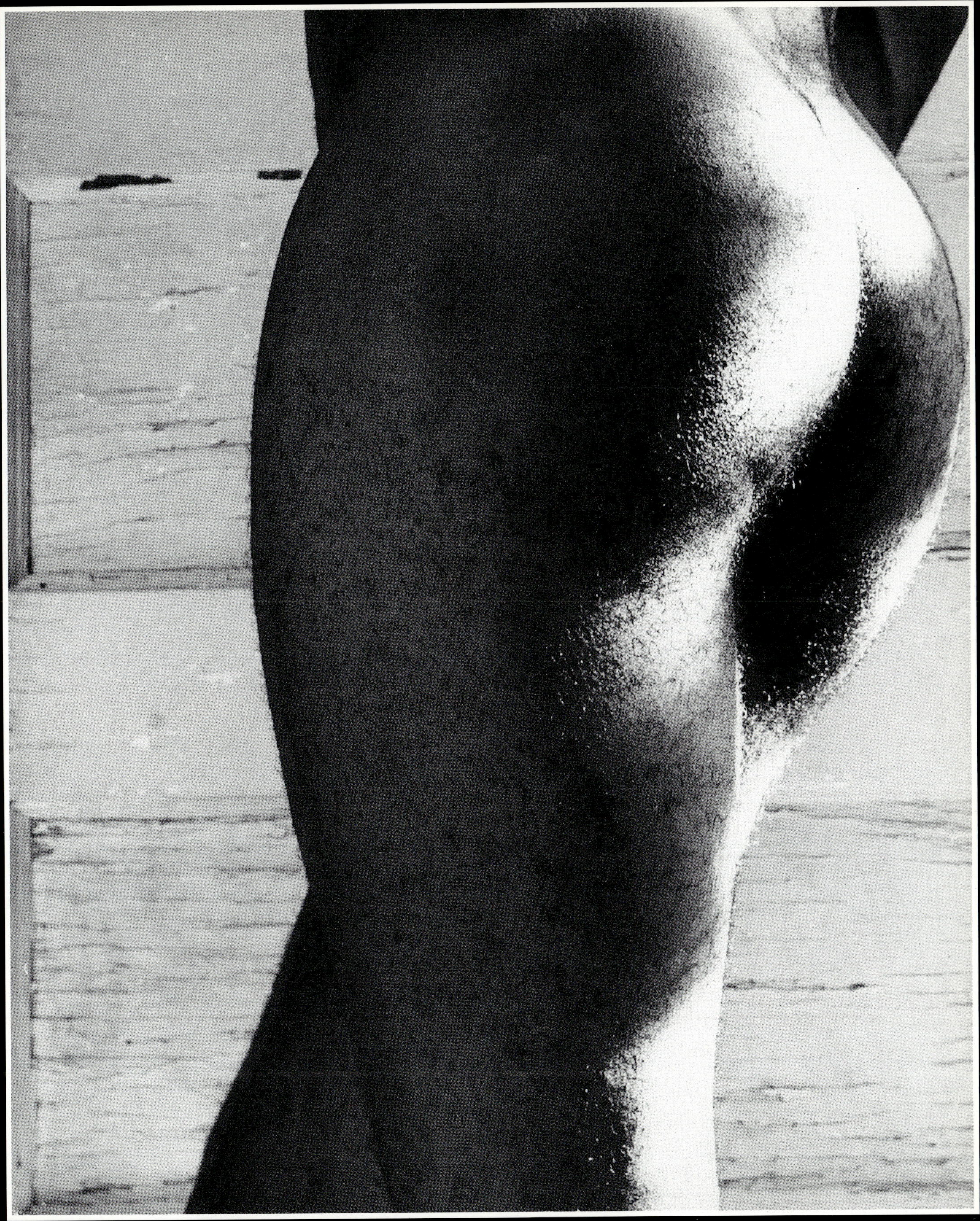

Robbin

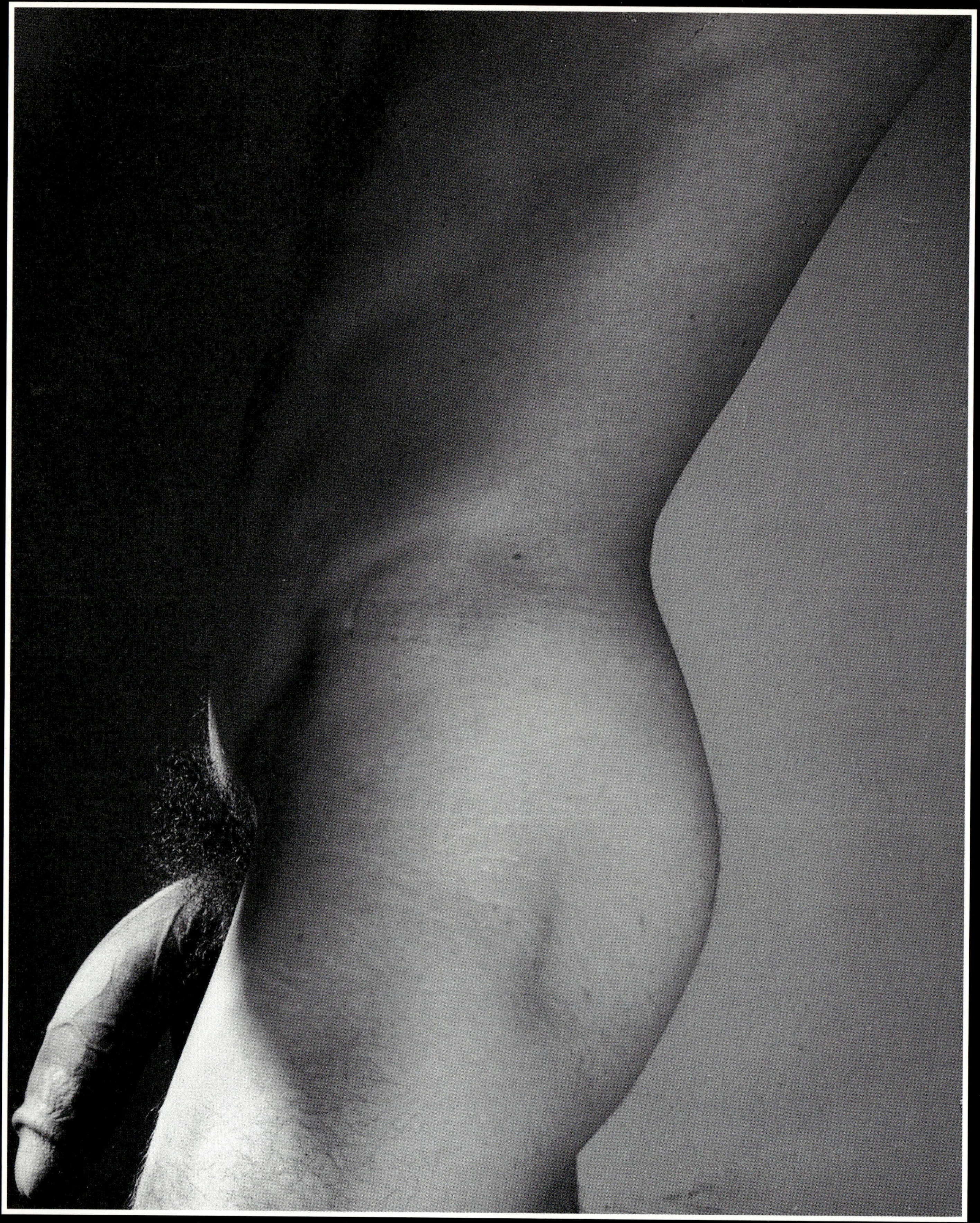

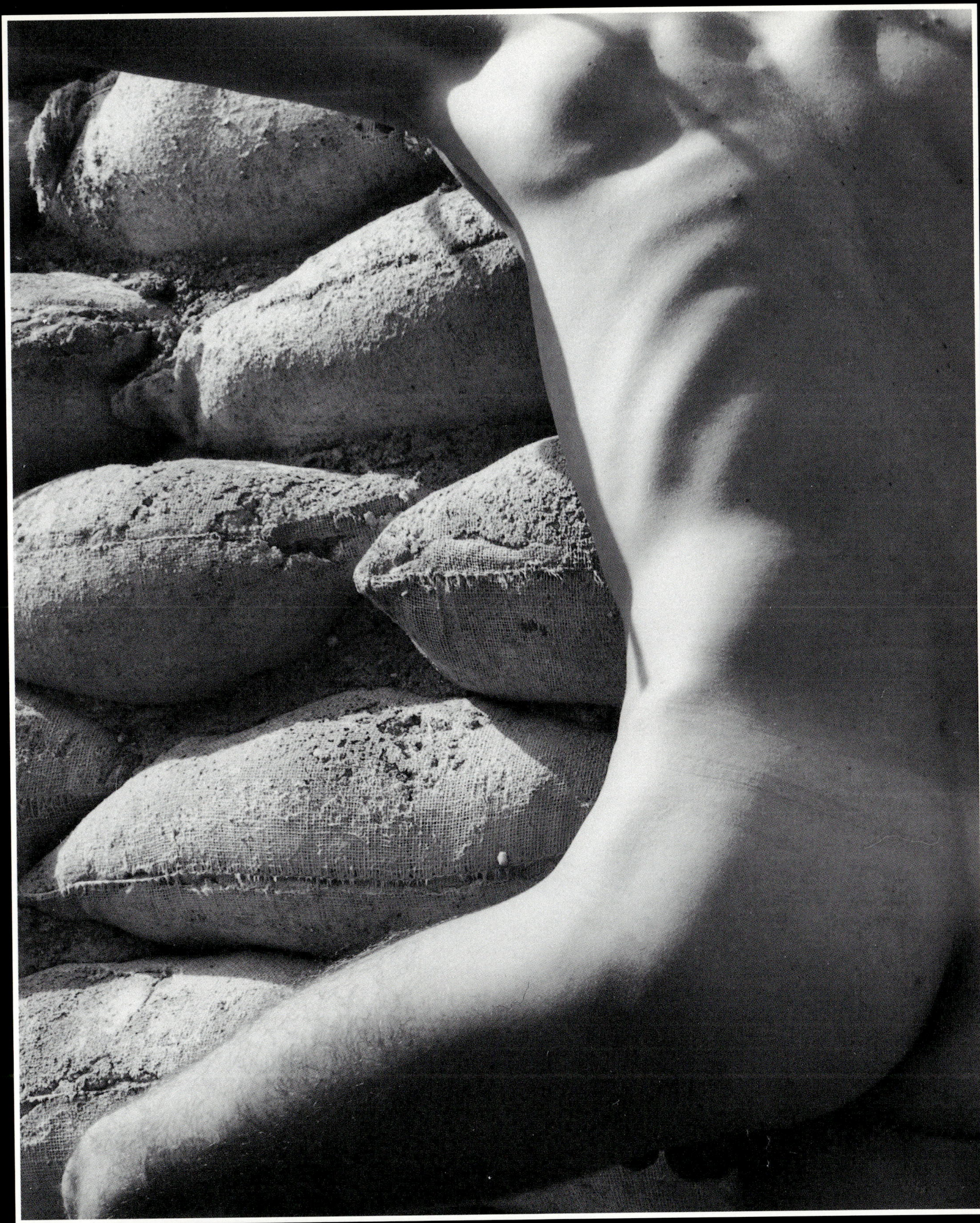

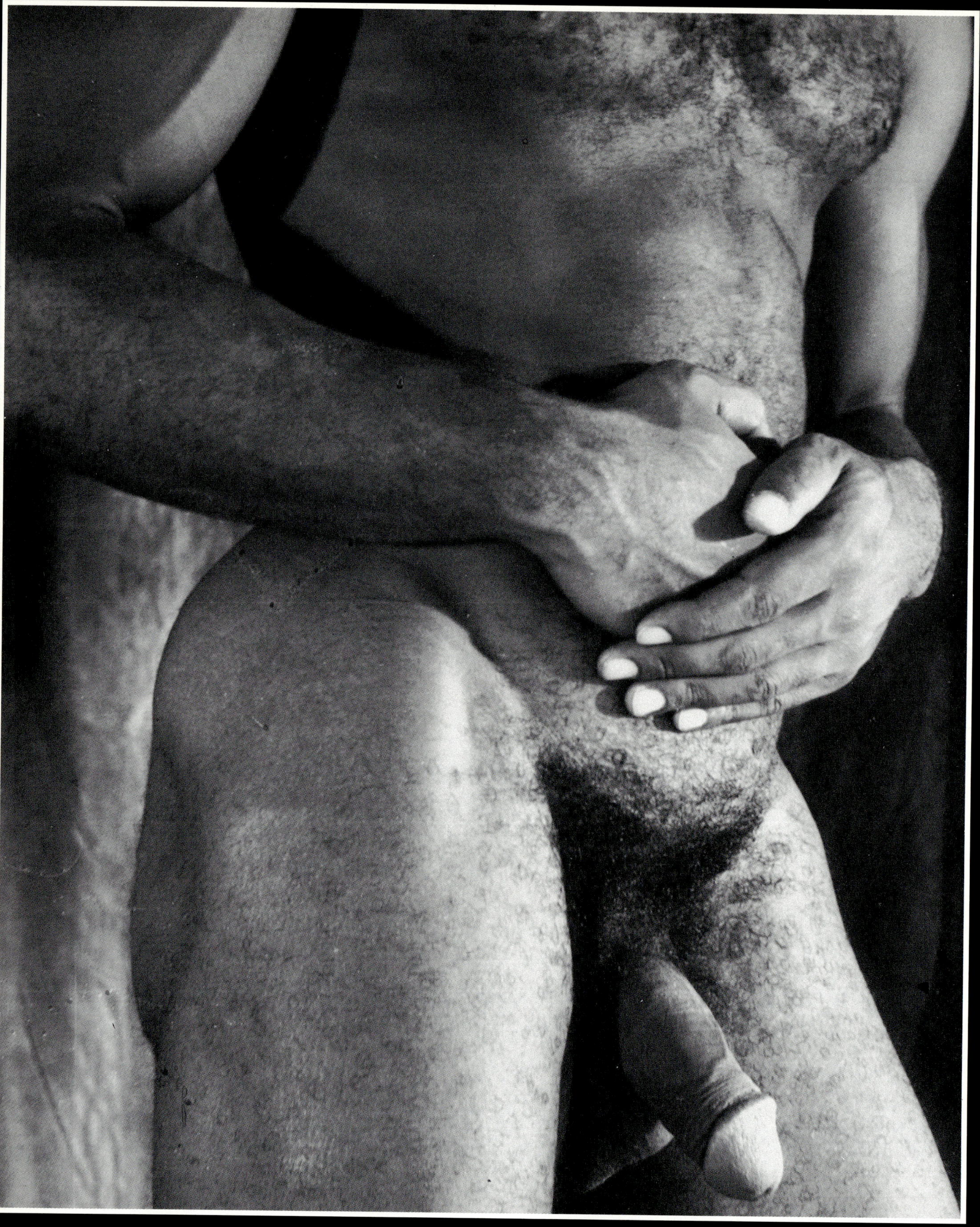

 Stephen

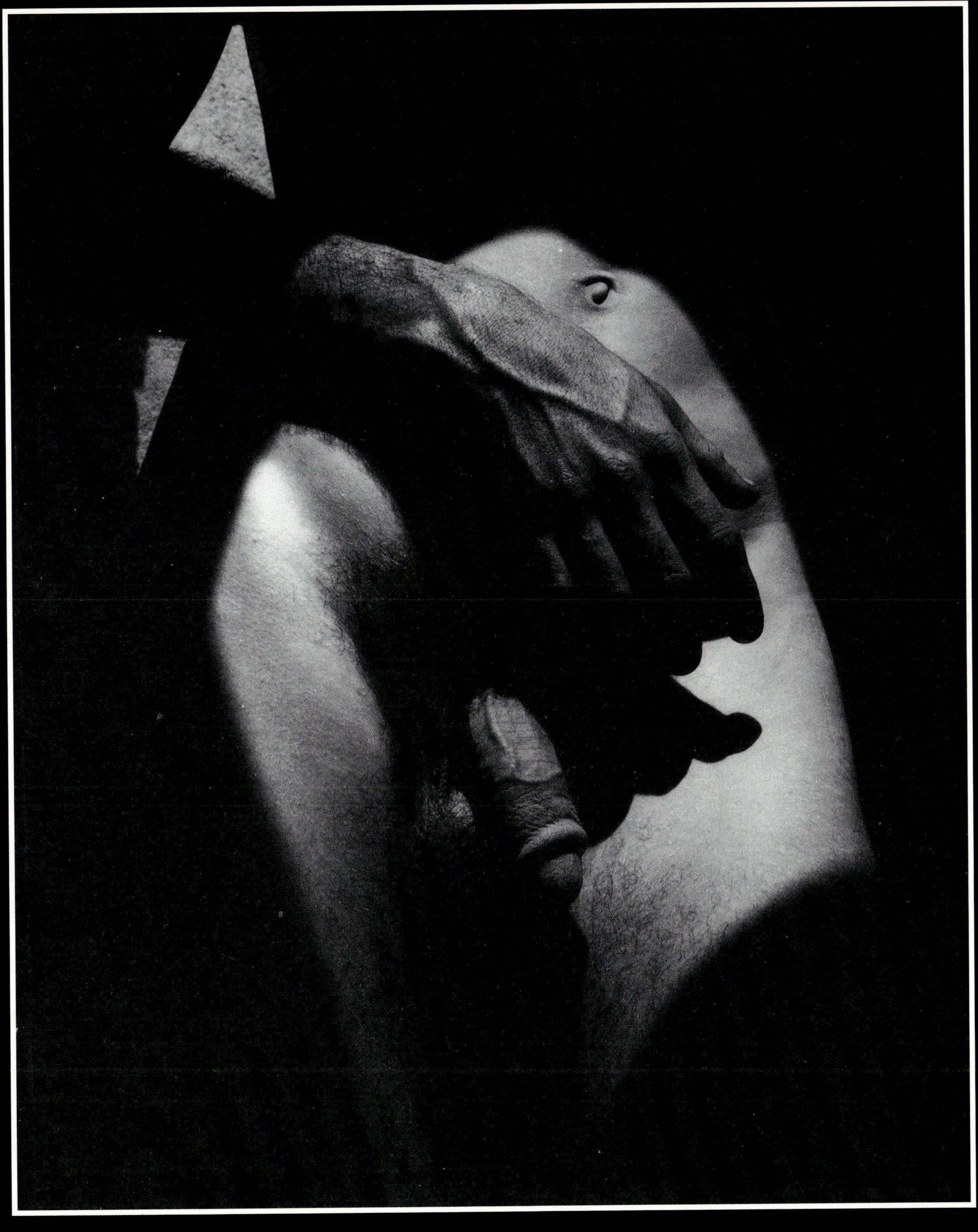

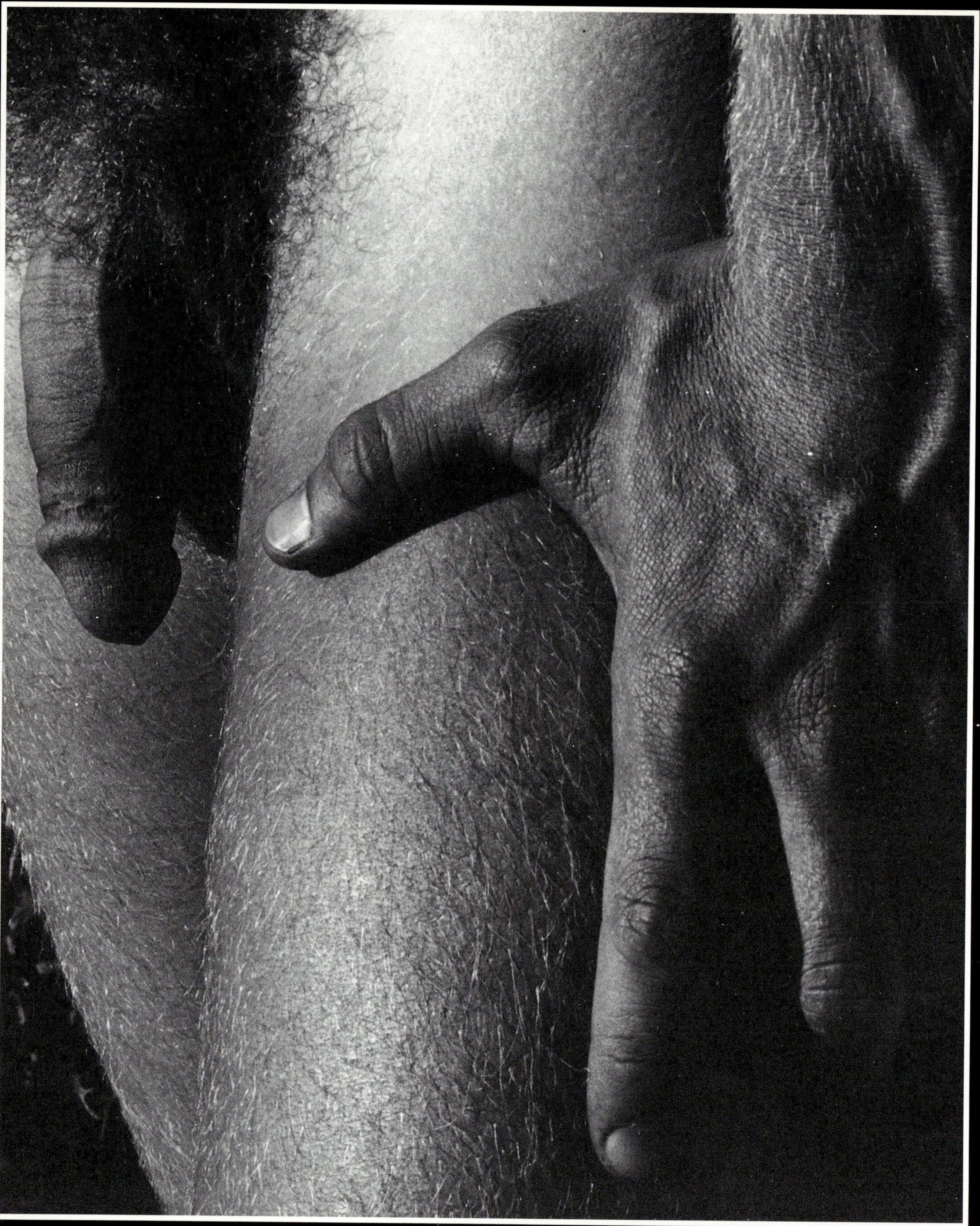

David

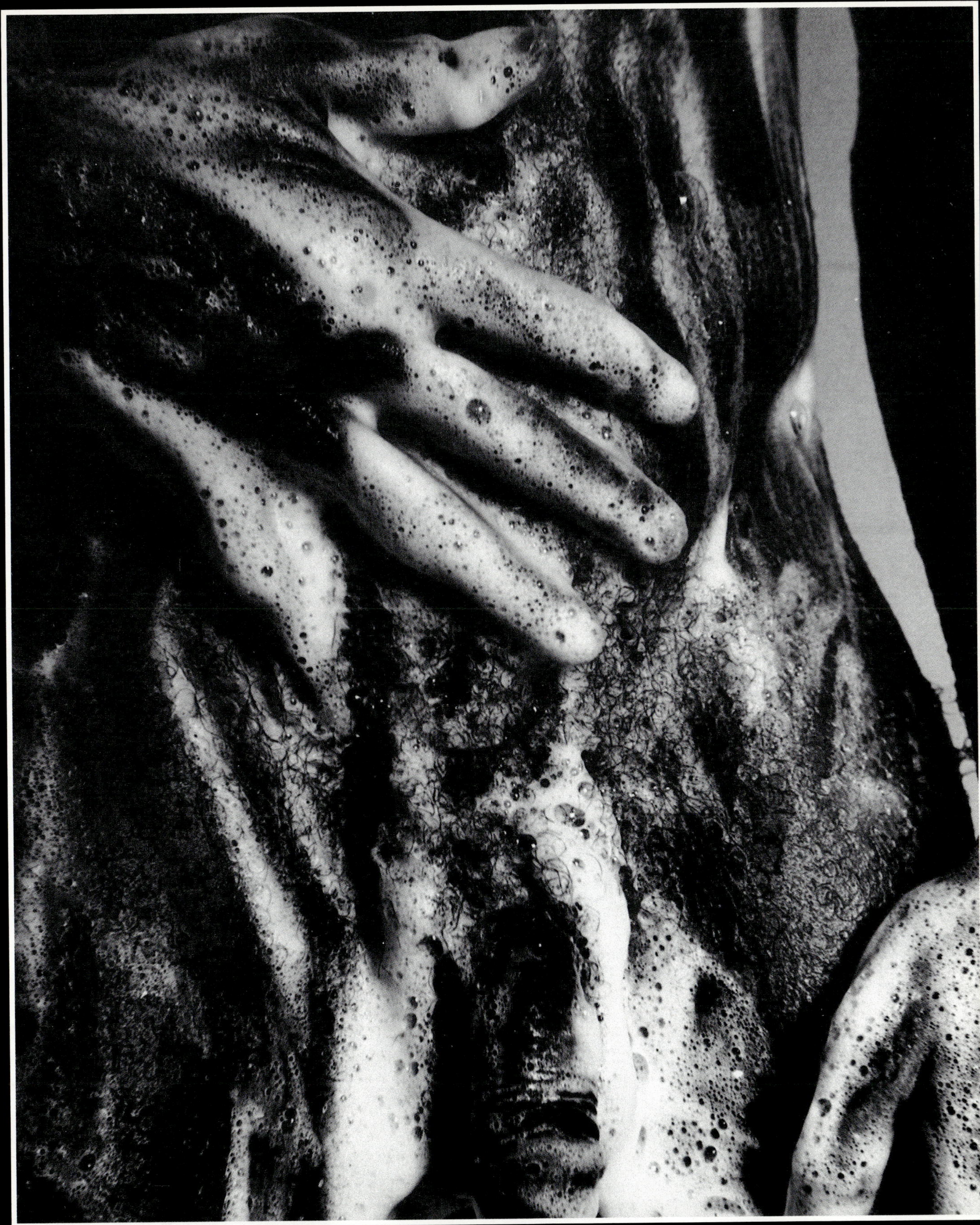

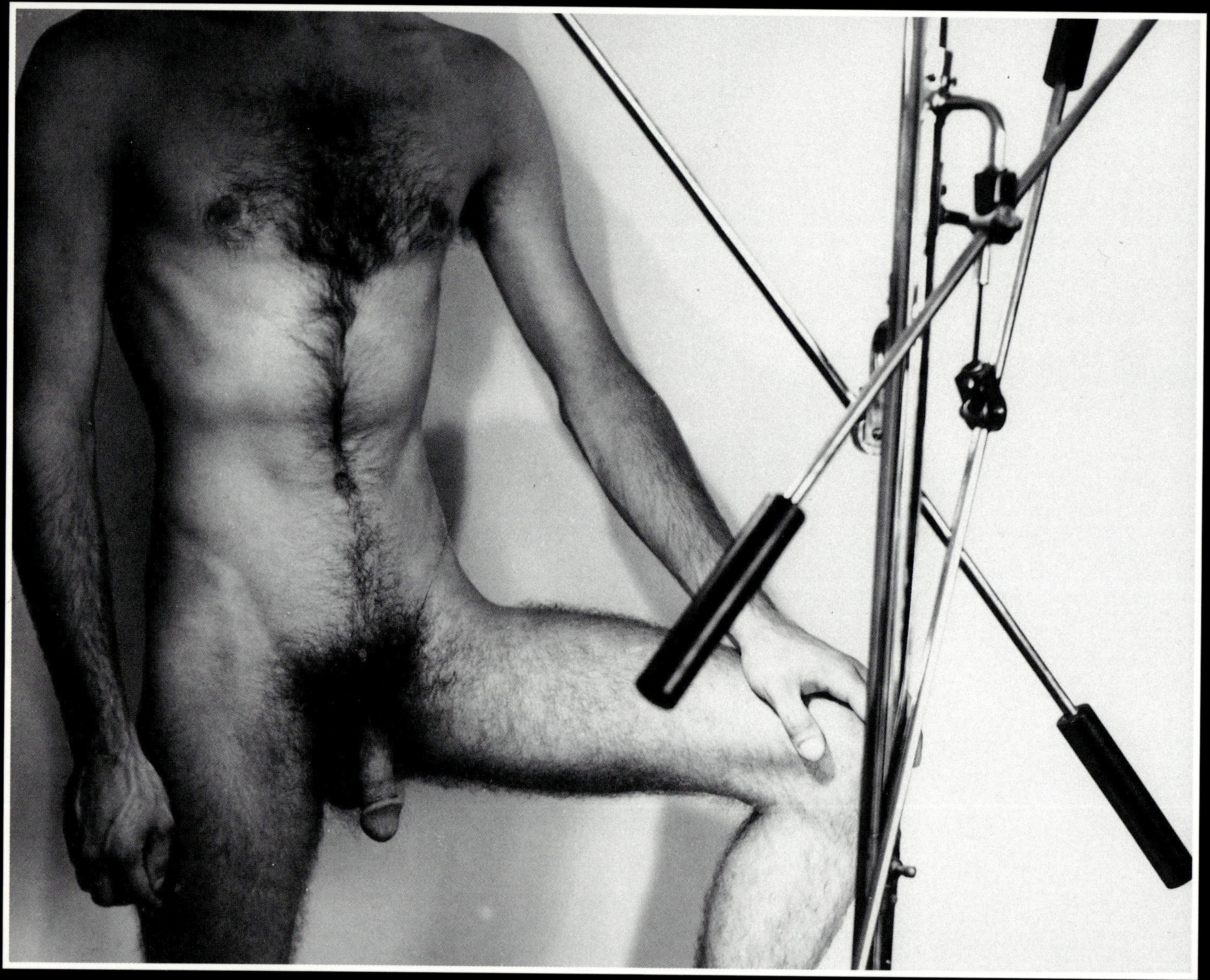

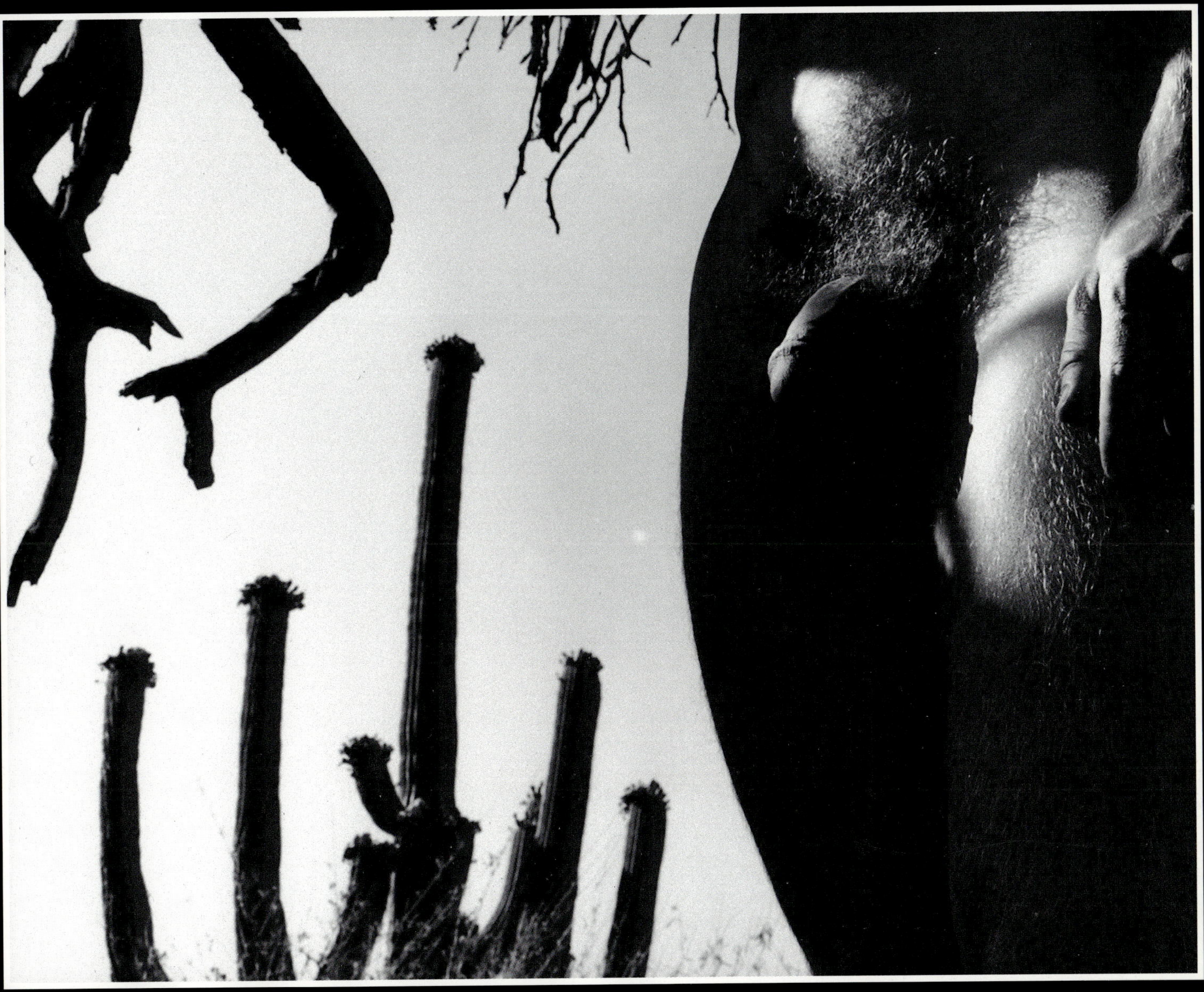

David

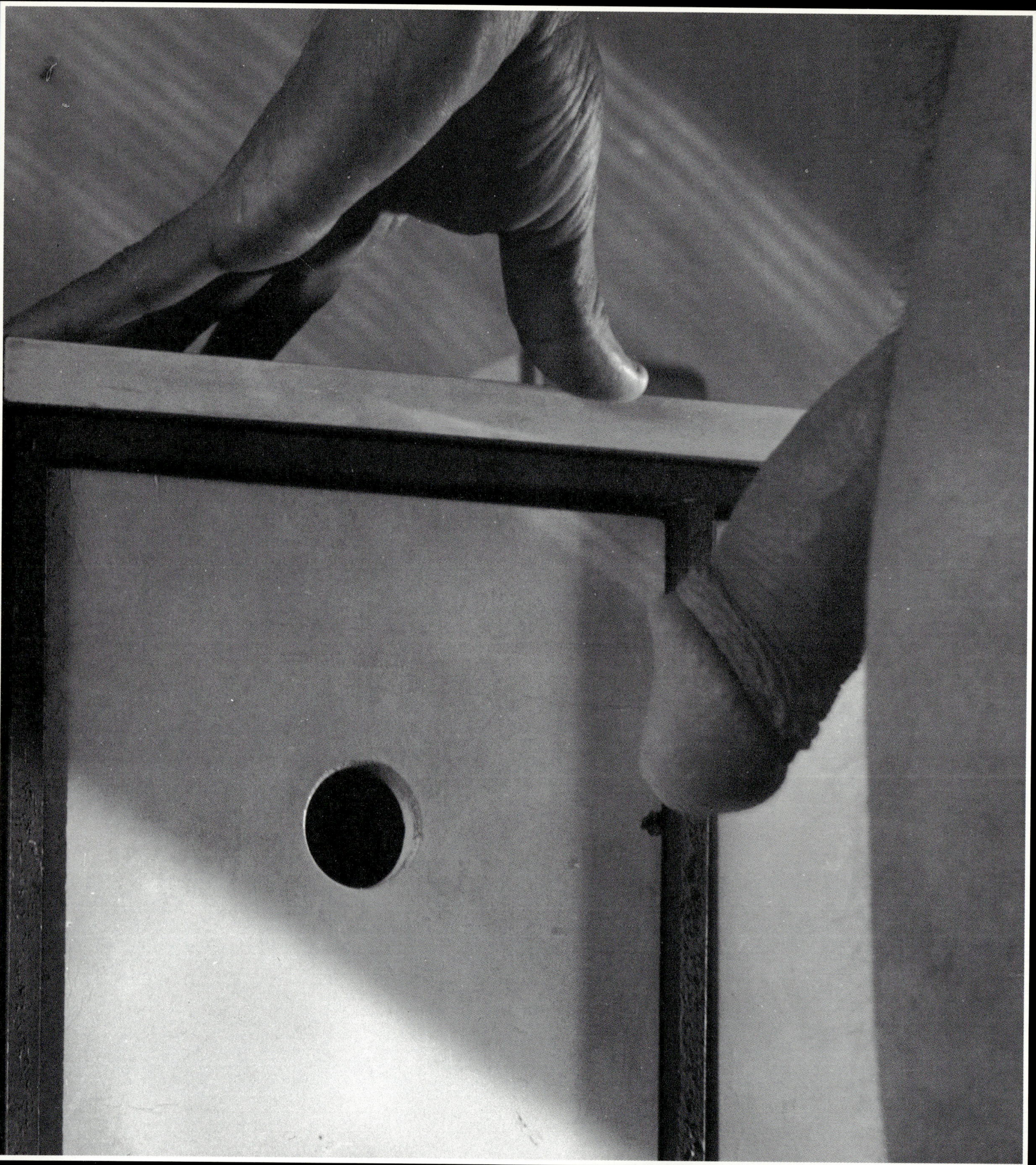

 Mike L

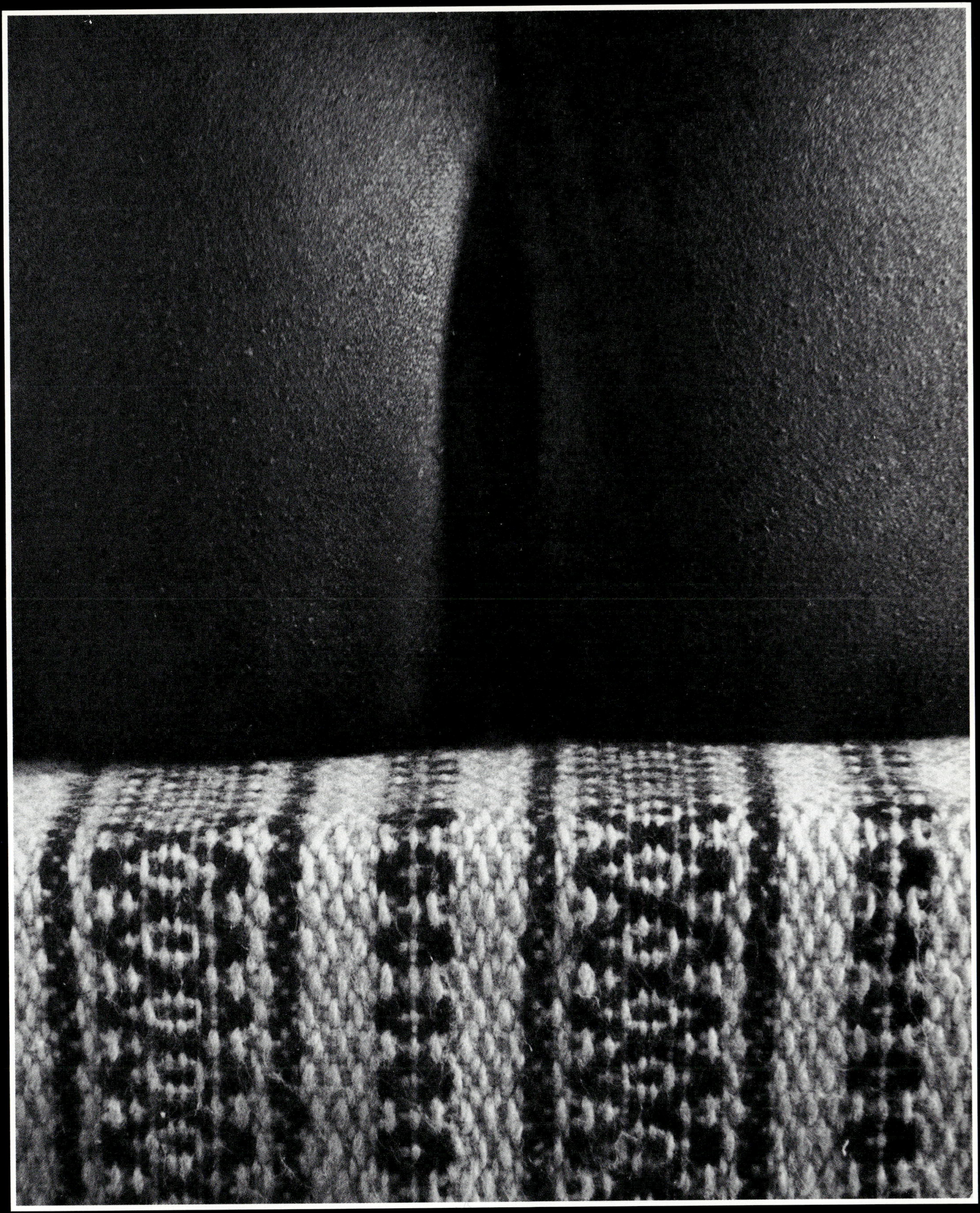

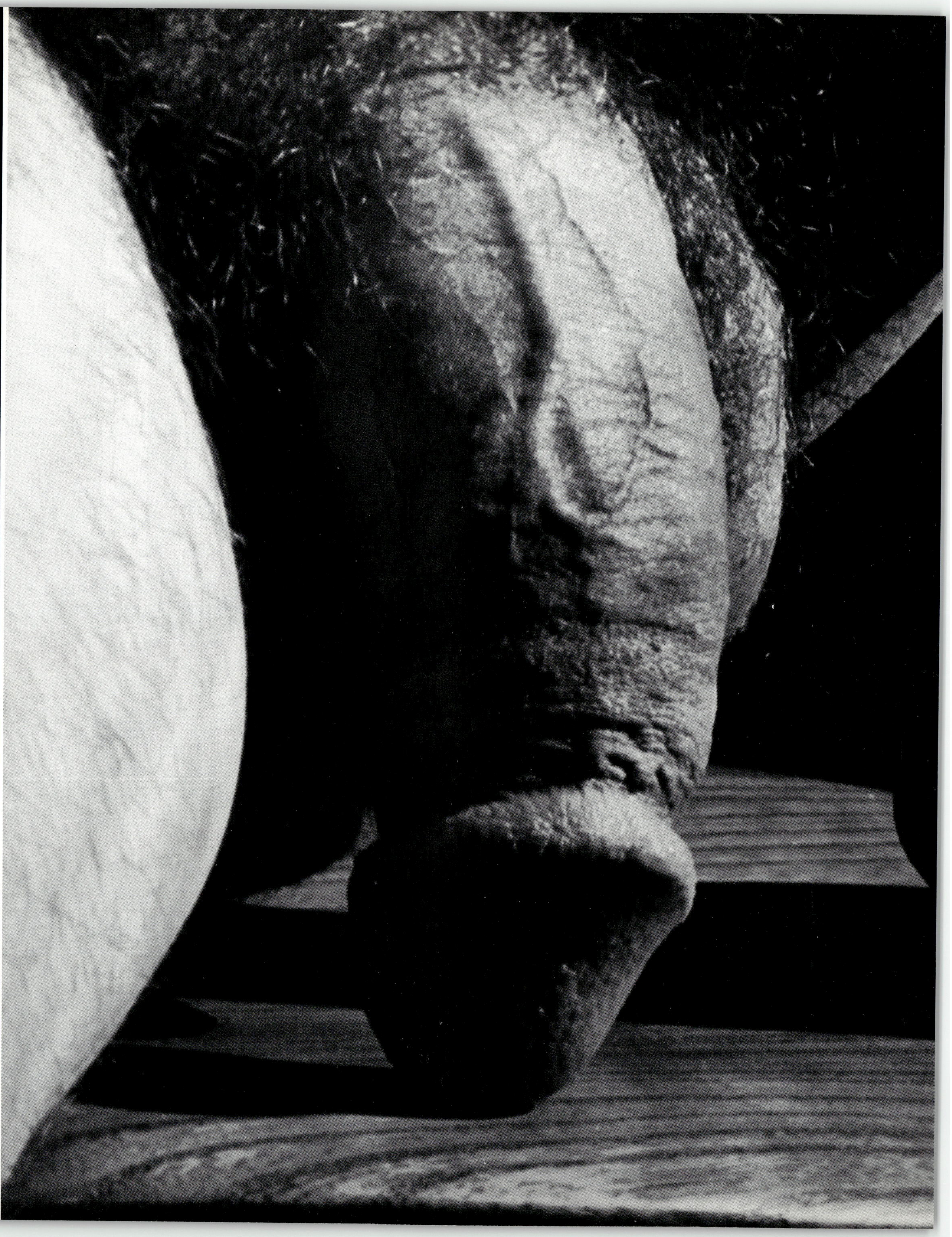

Tony

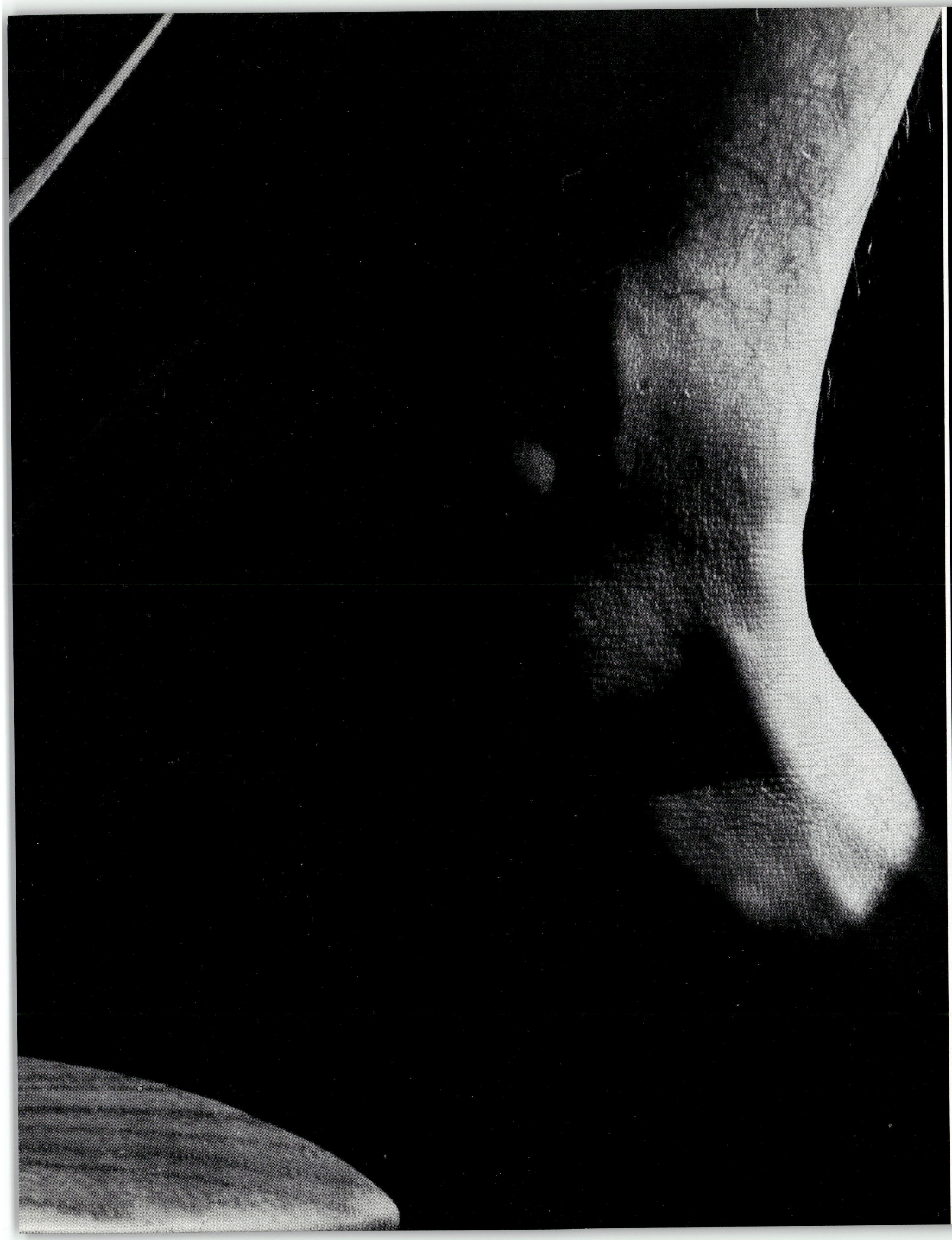

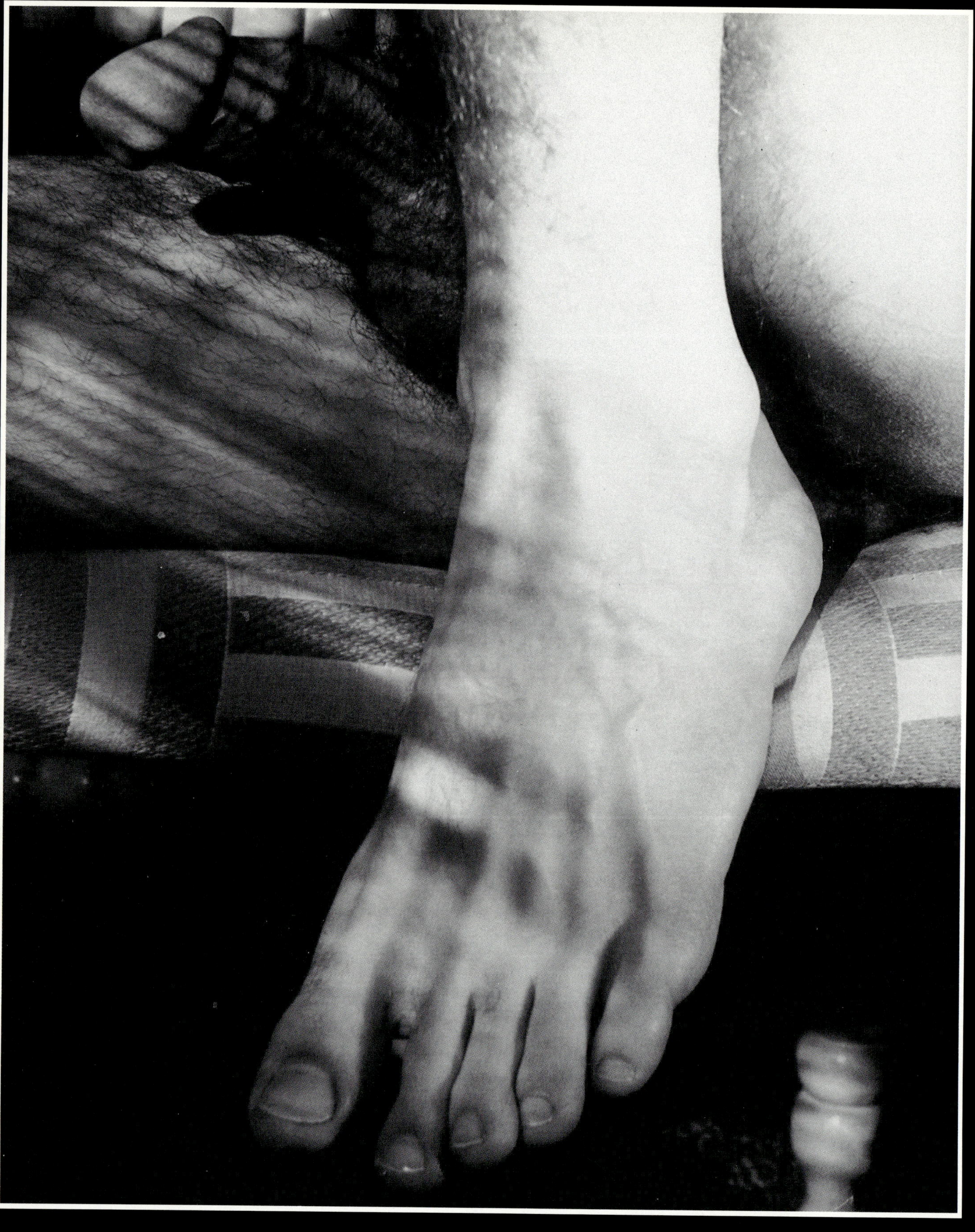

 Mike C

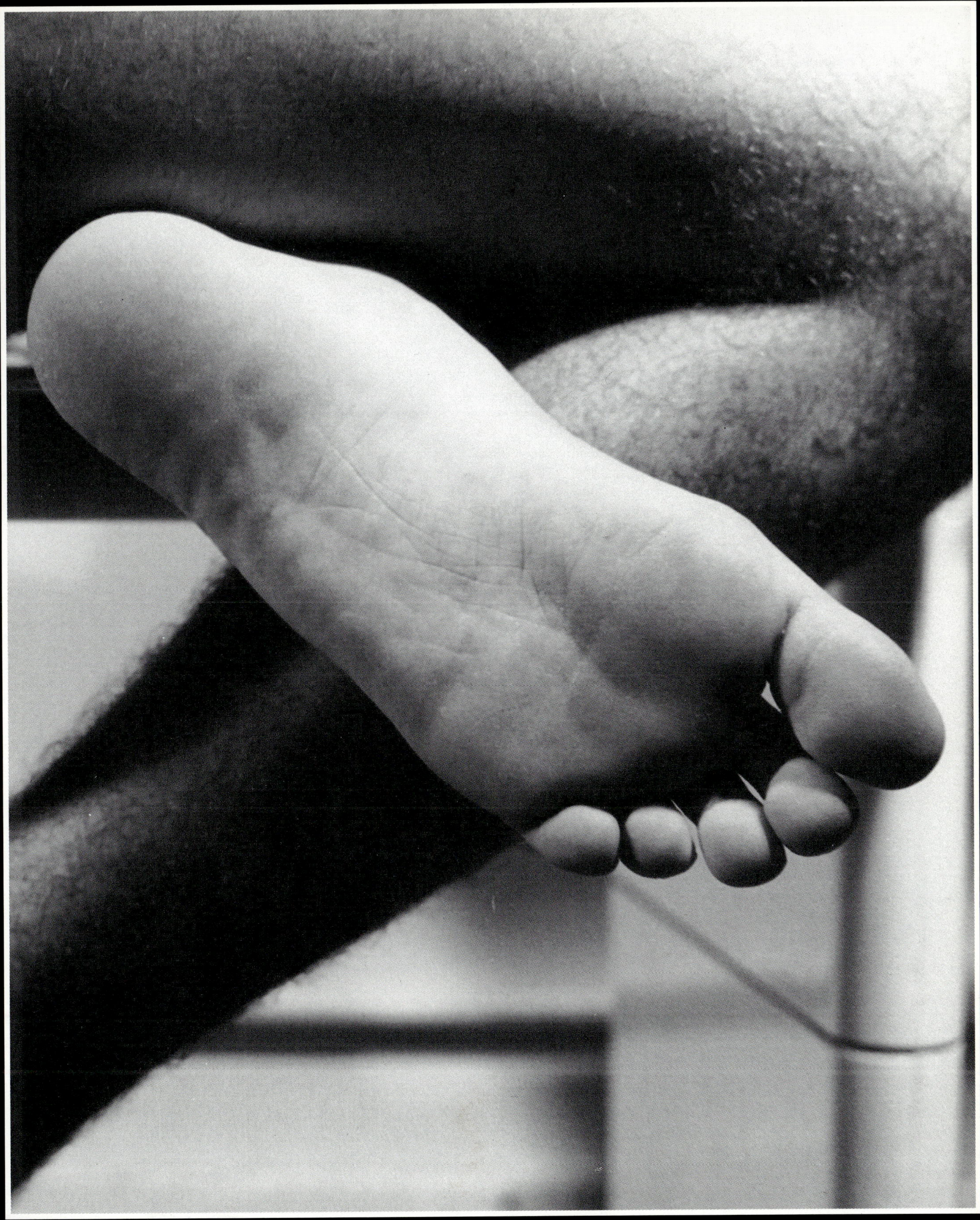

John

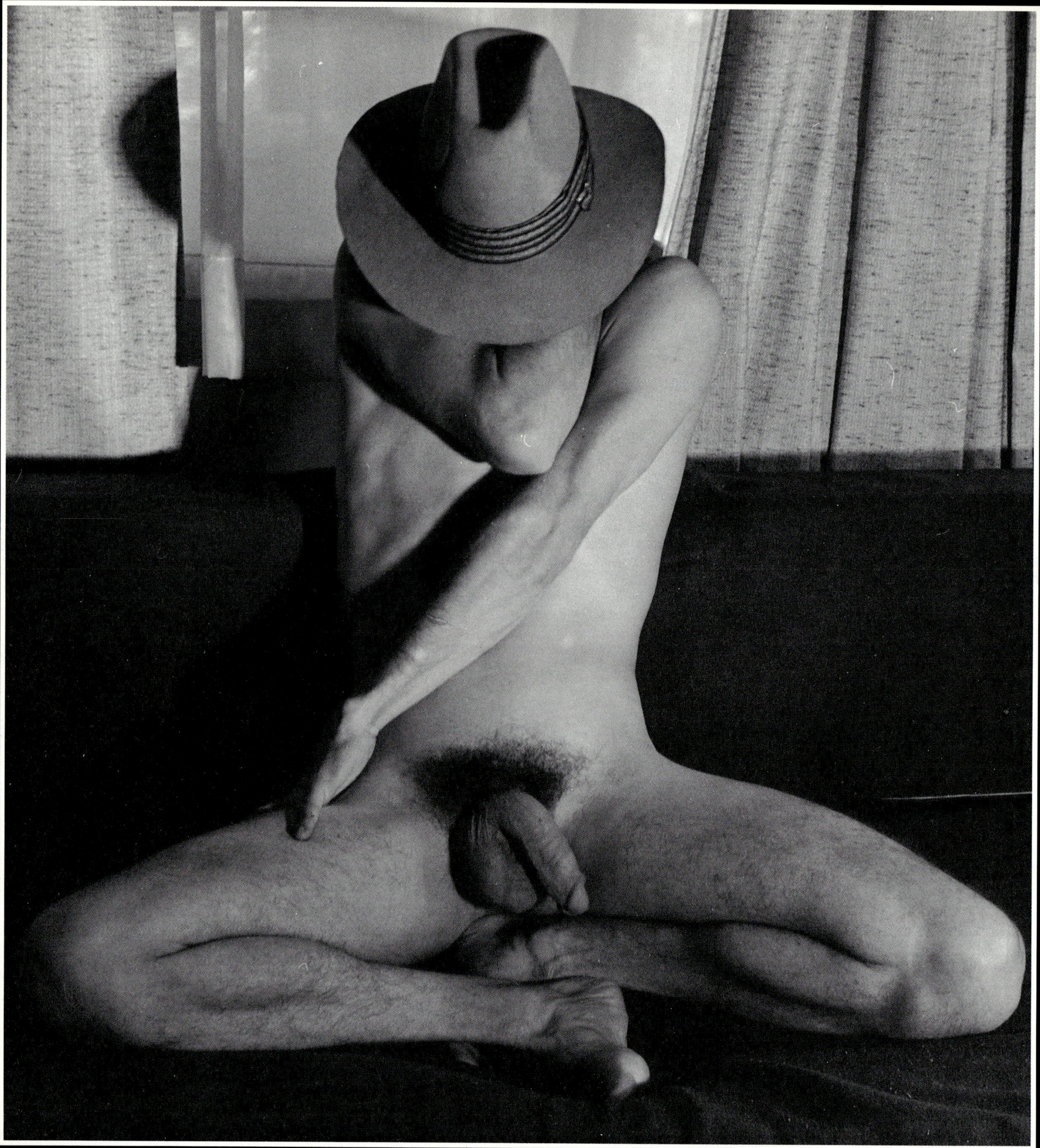

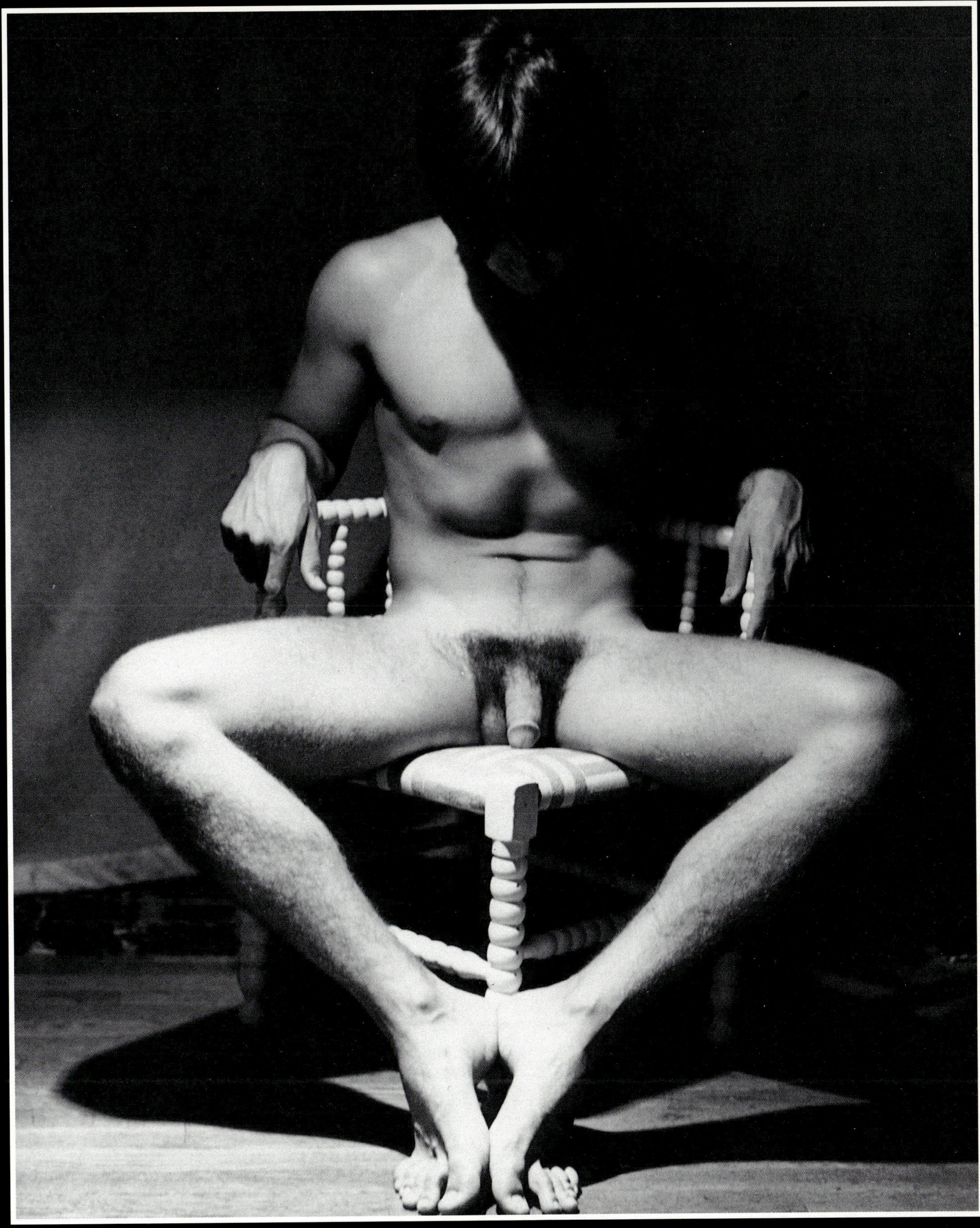

Sean

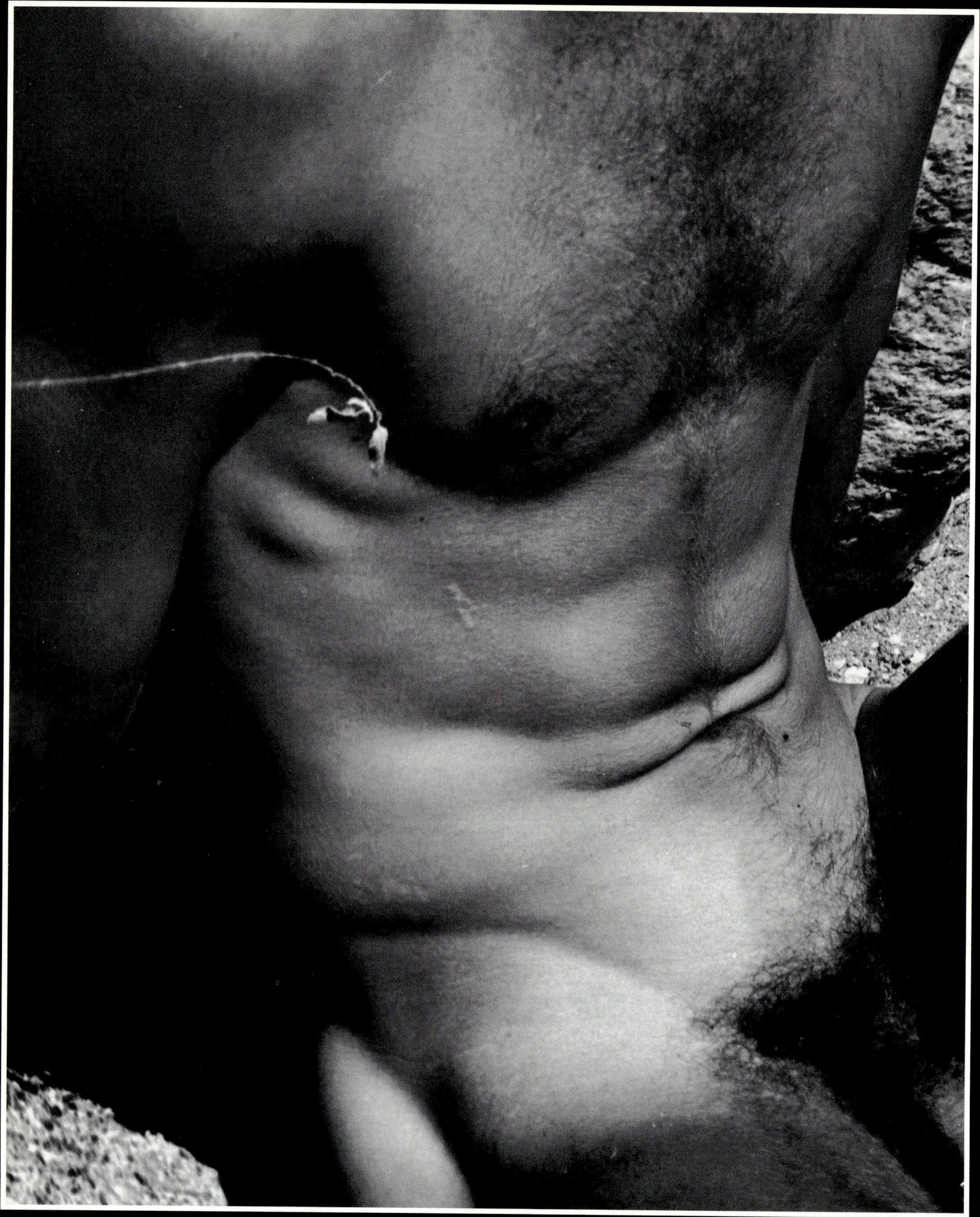

 David

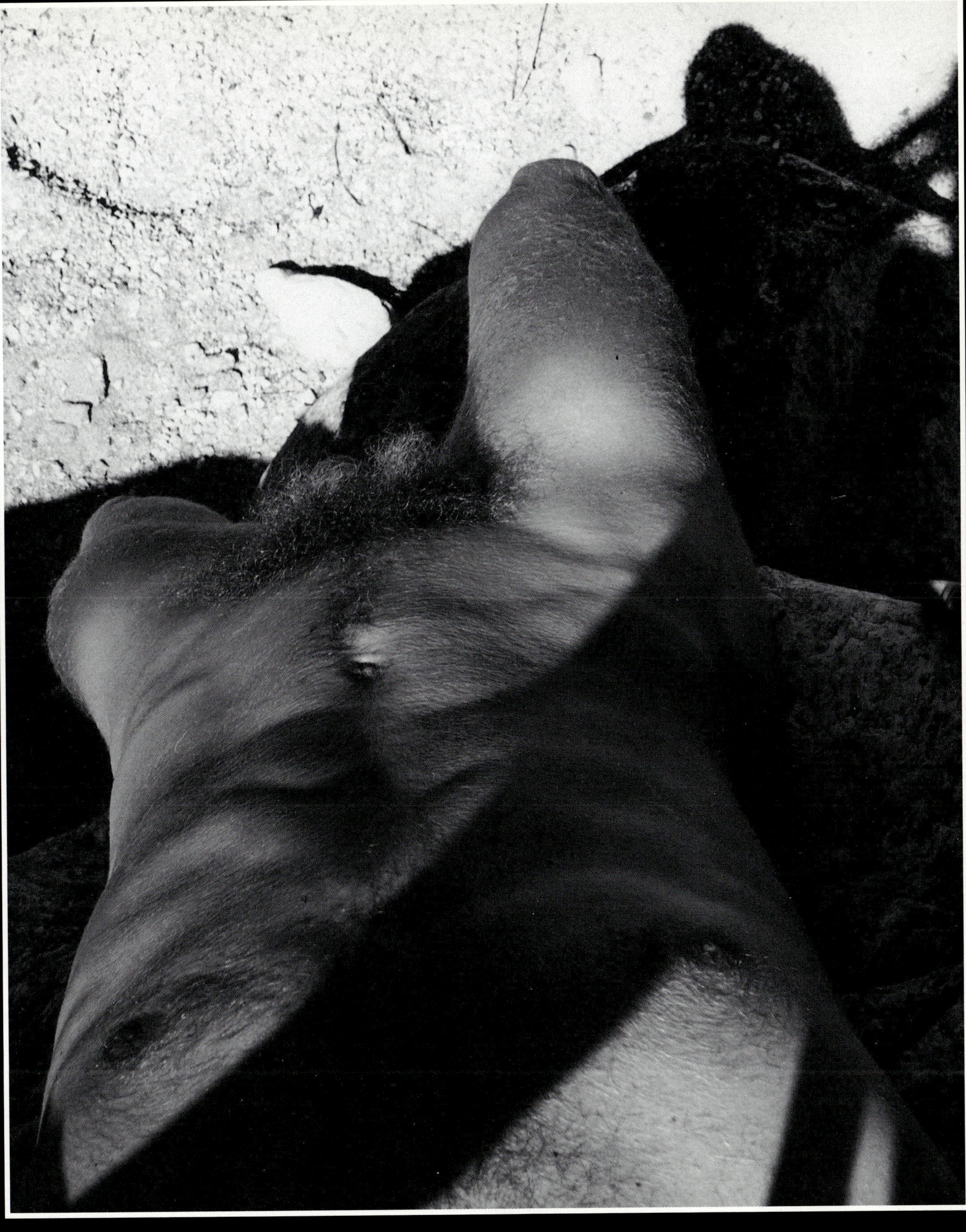

David

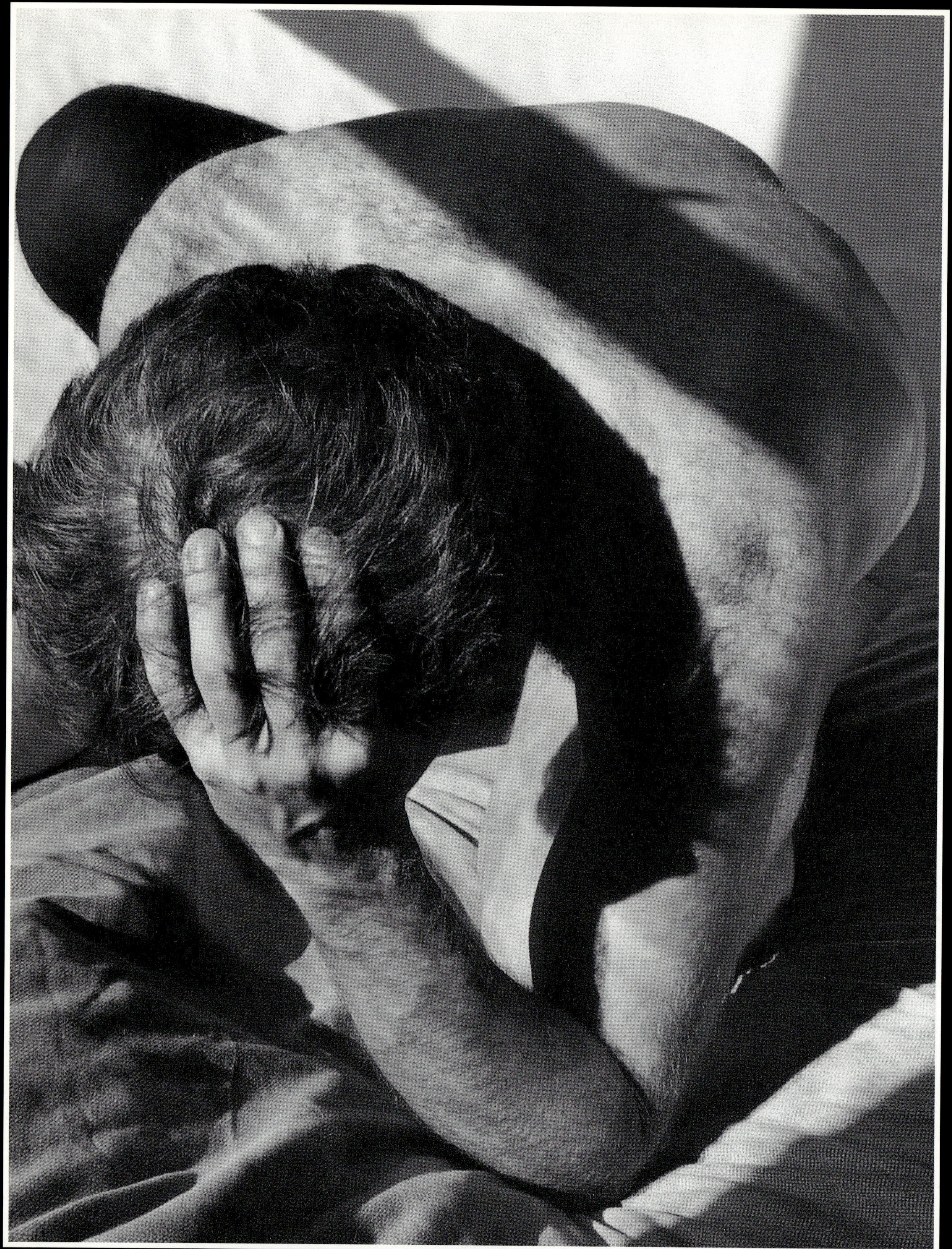

 George

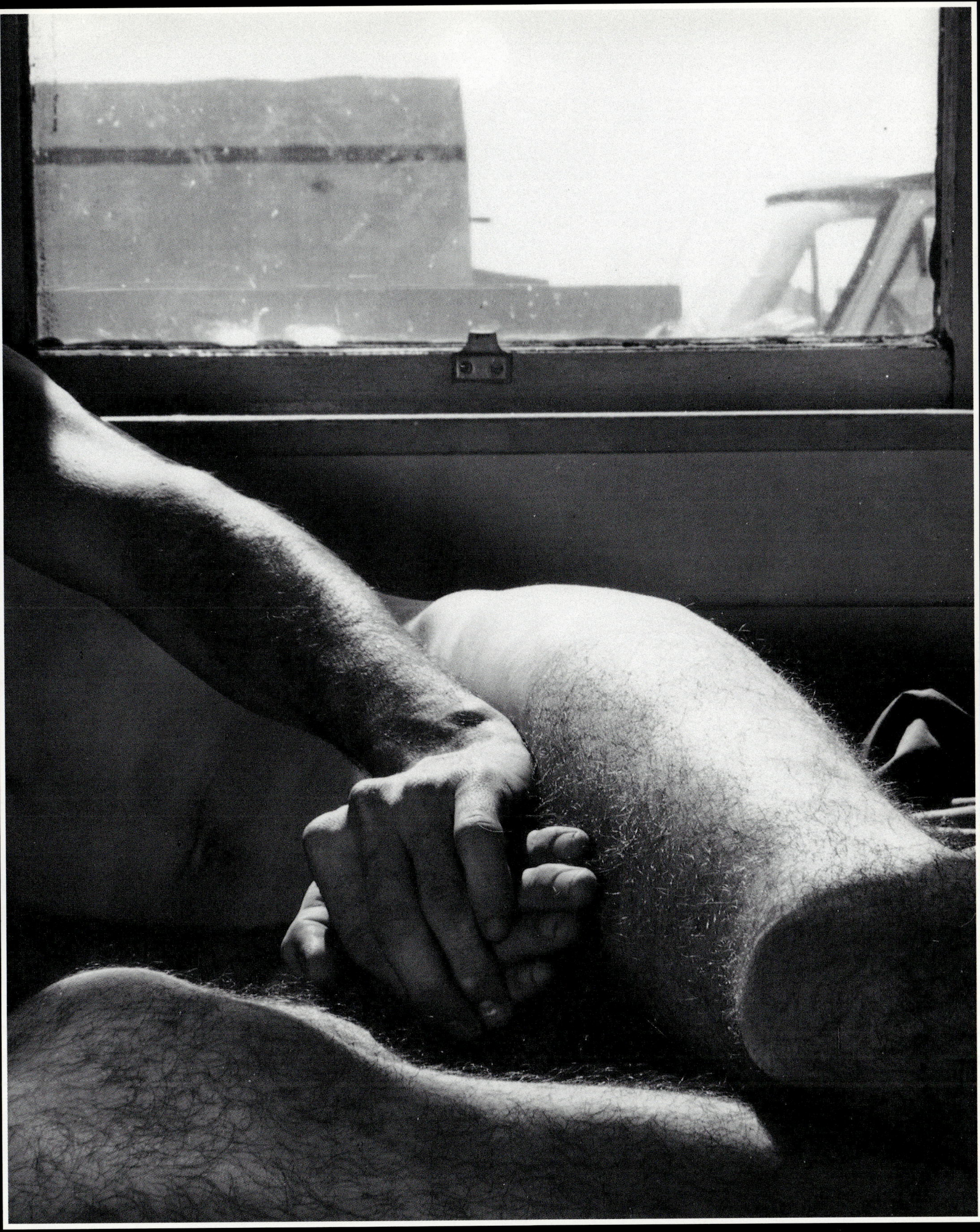

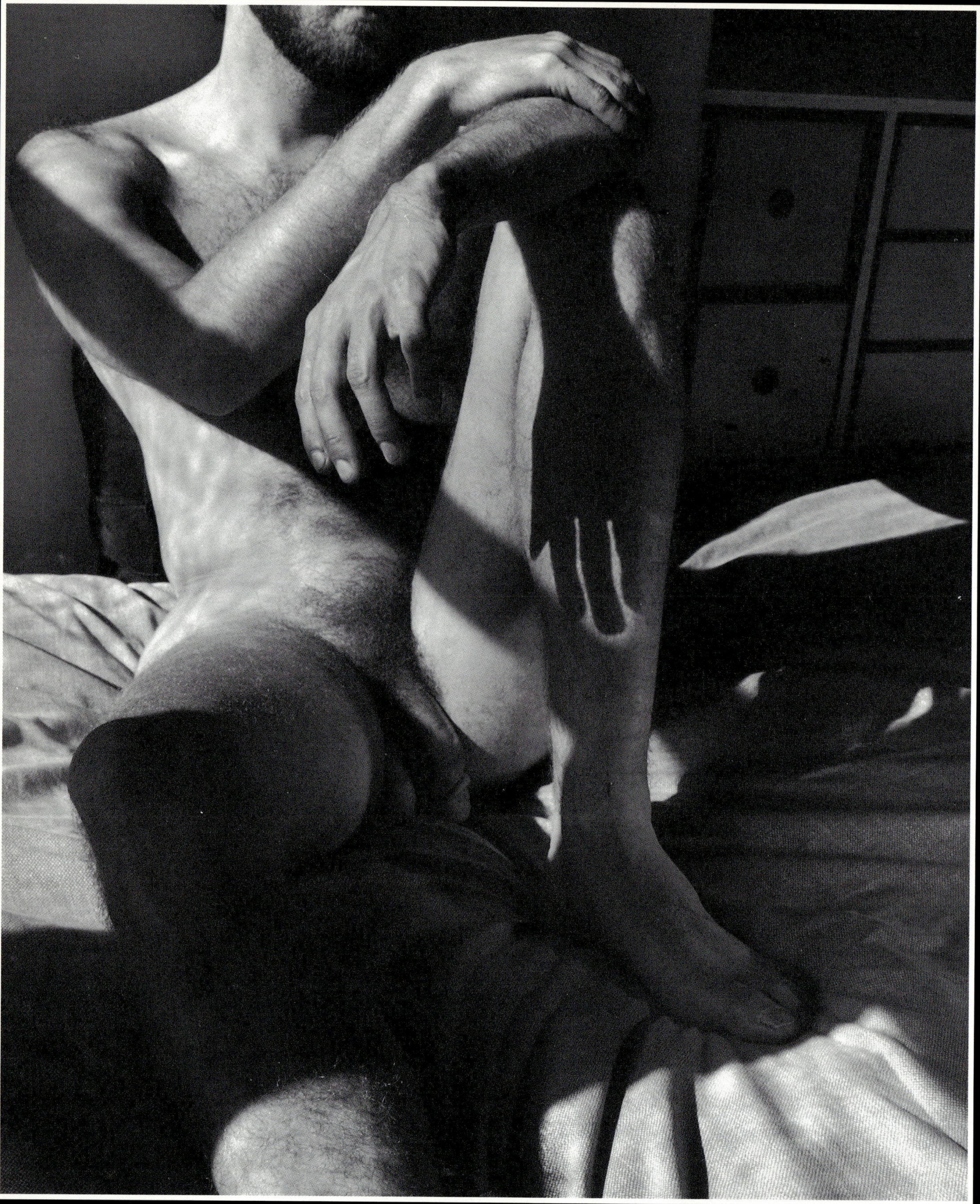

George

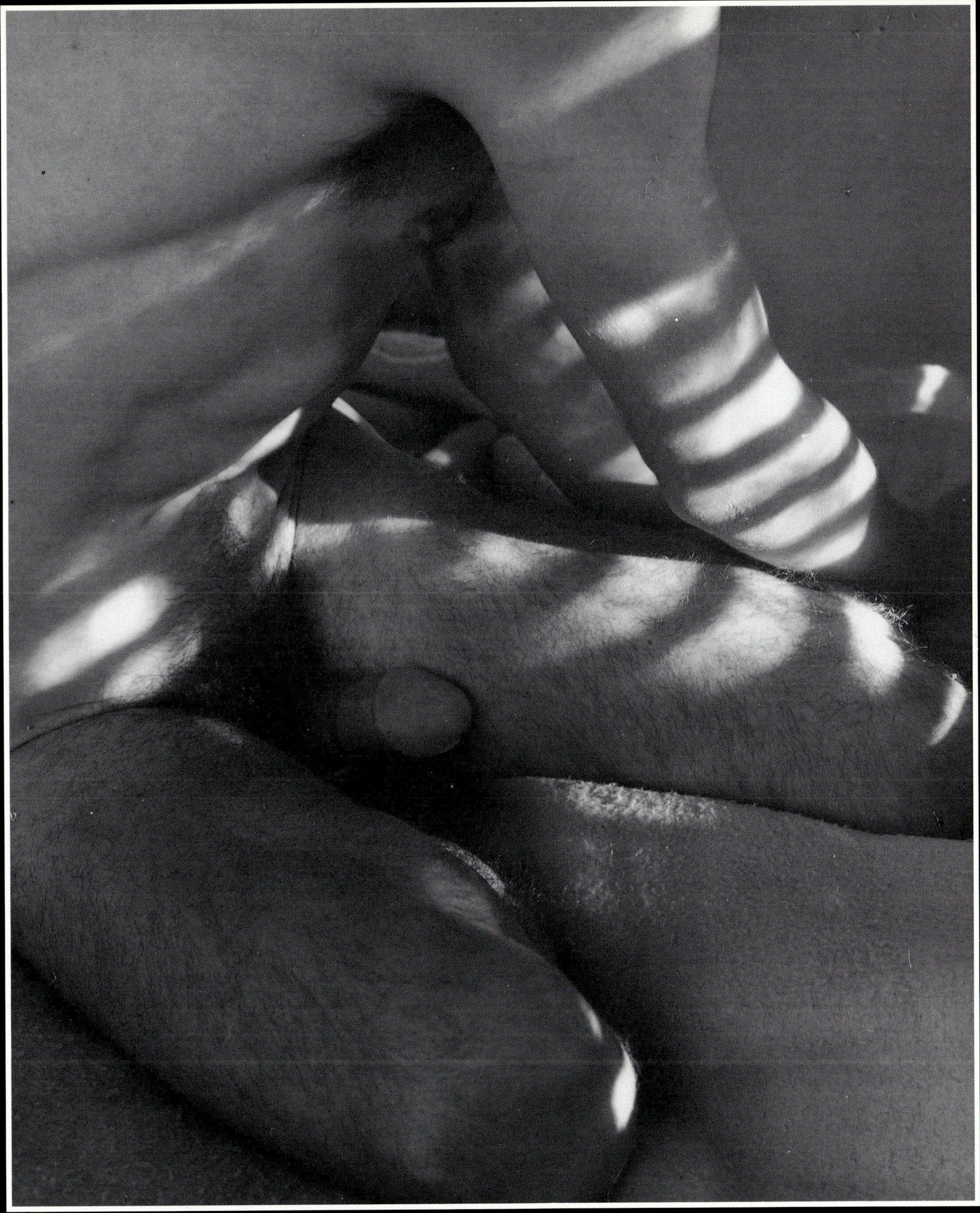

Mike C

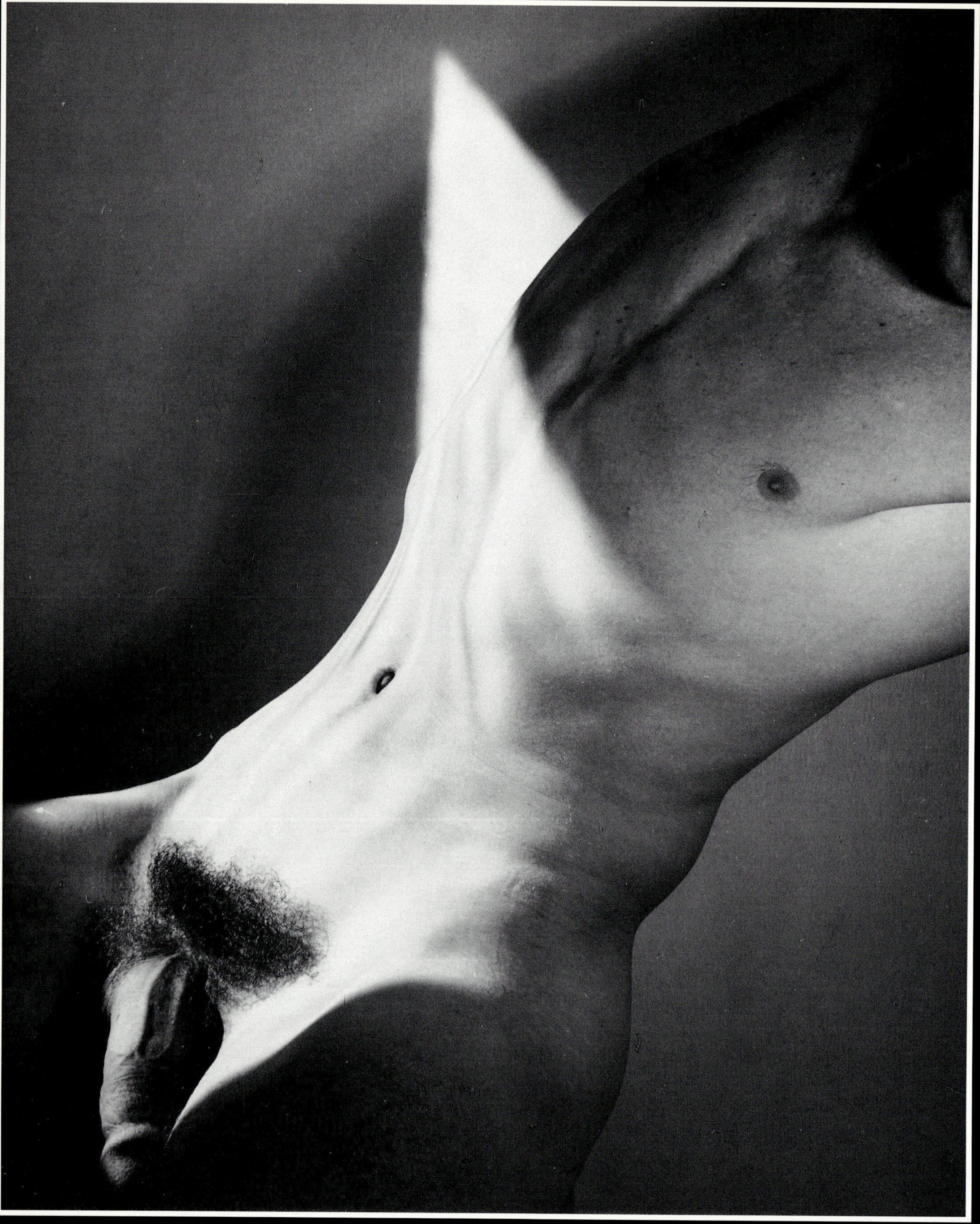

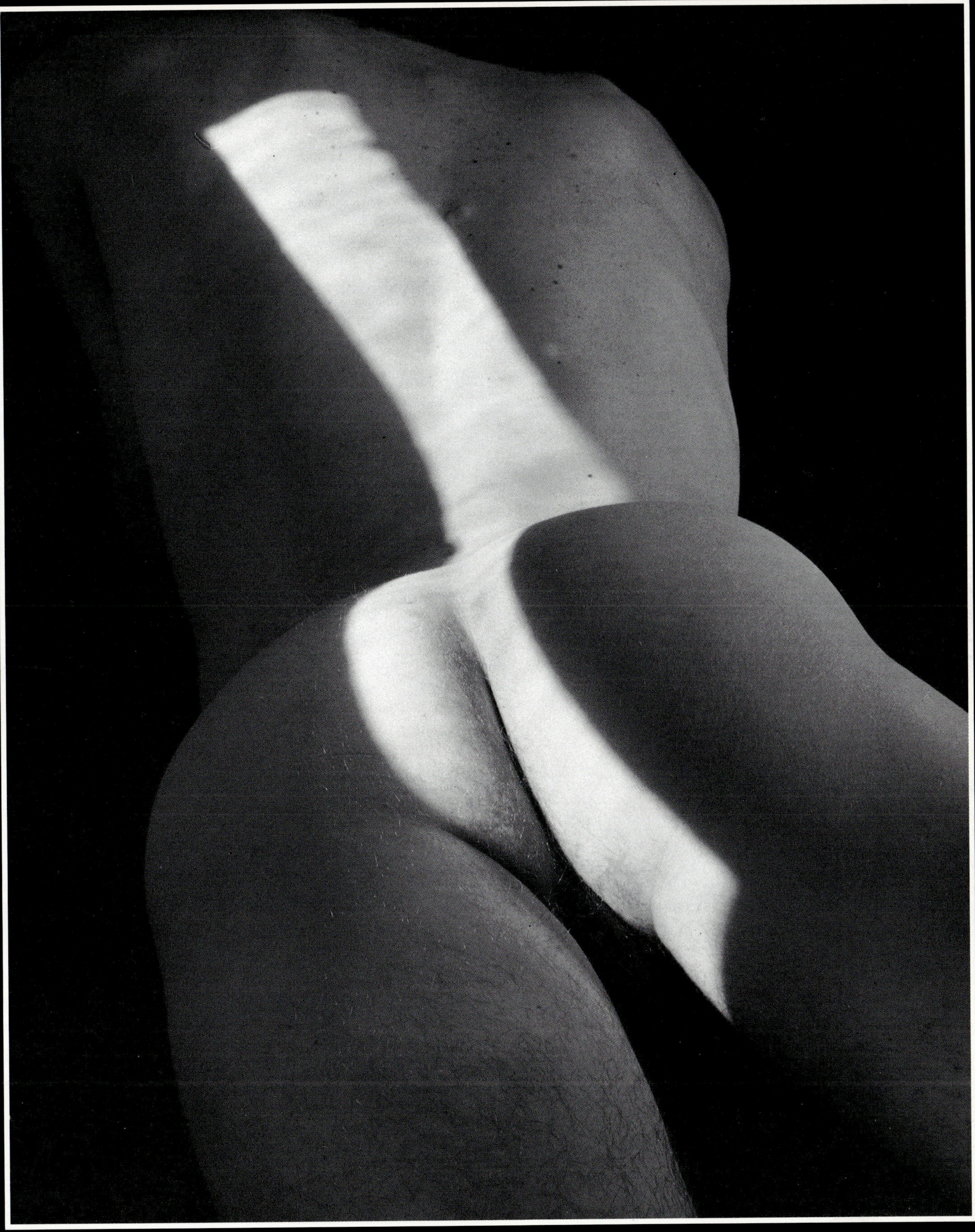

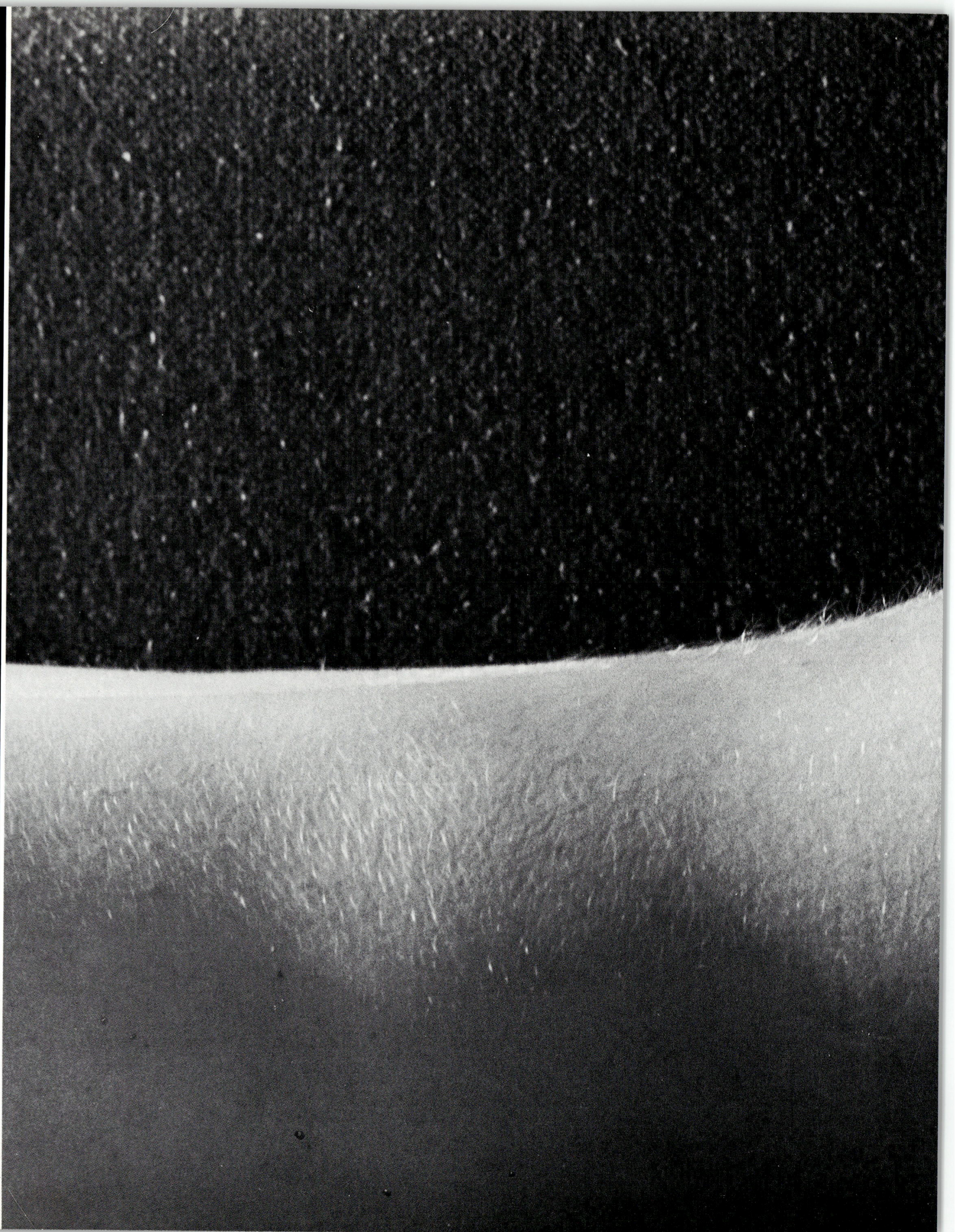

David

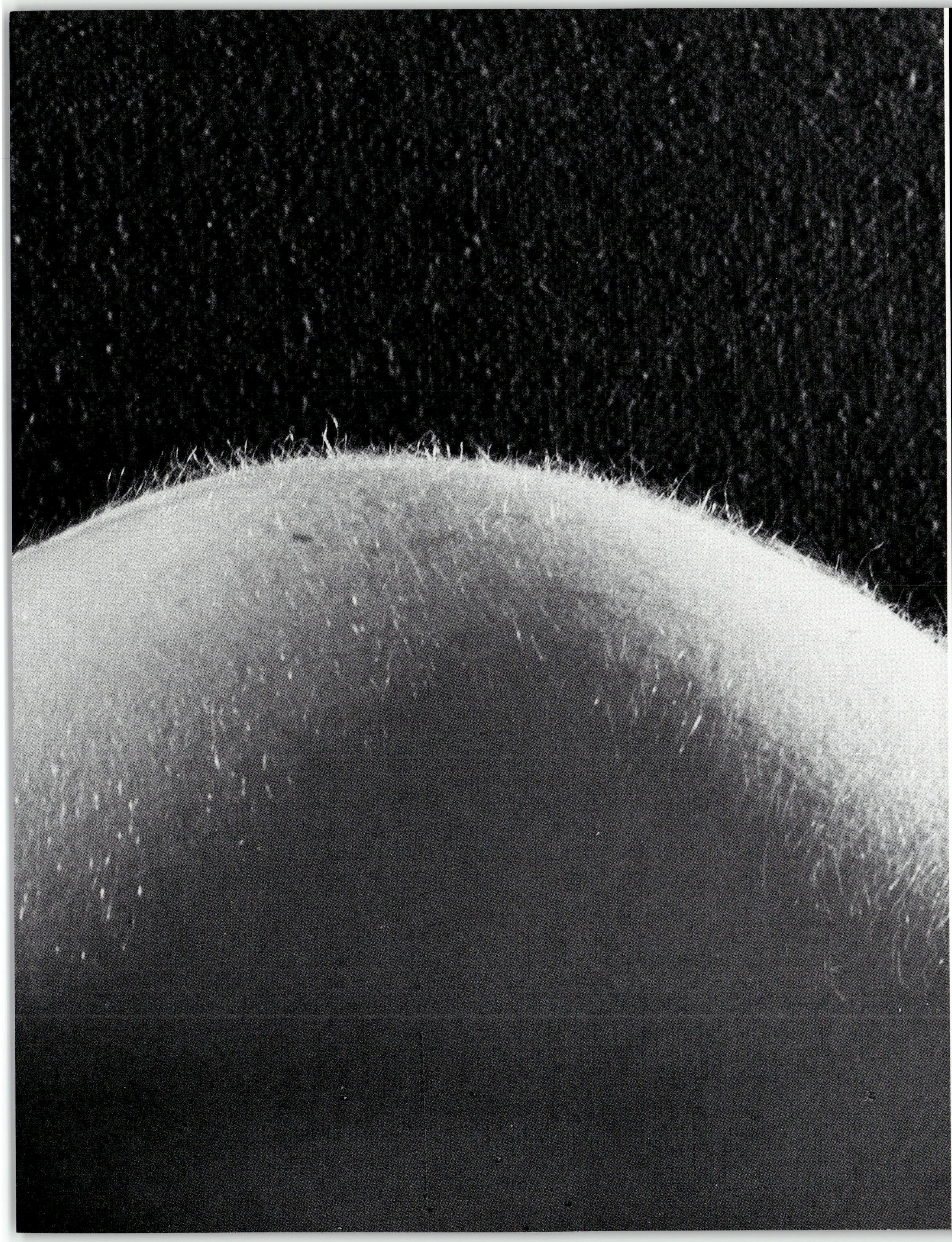

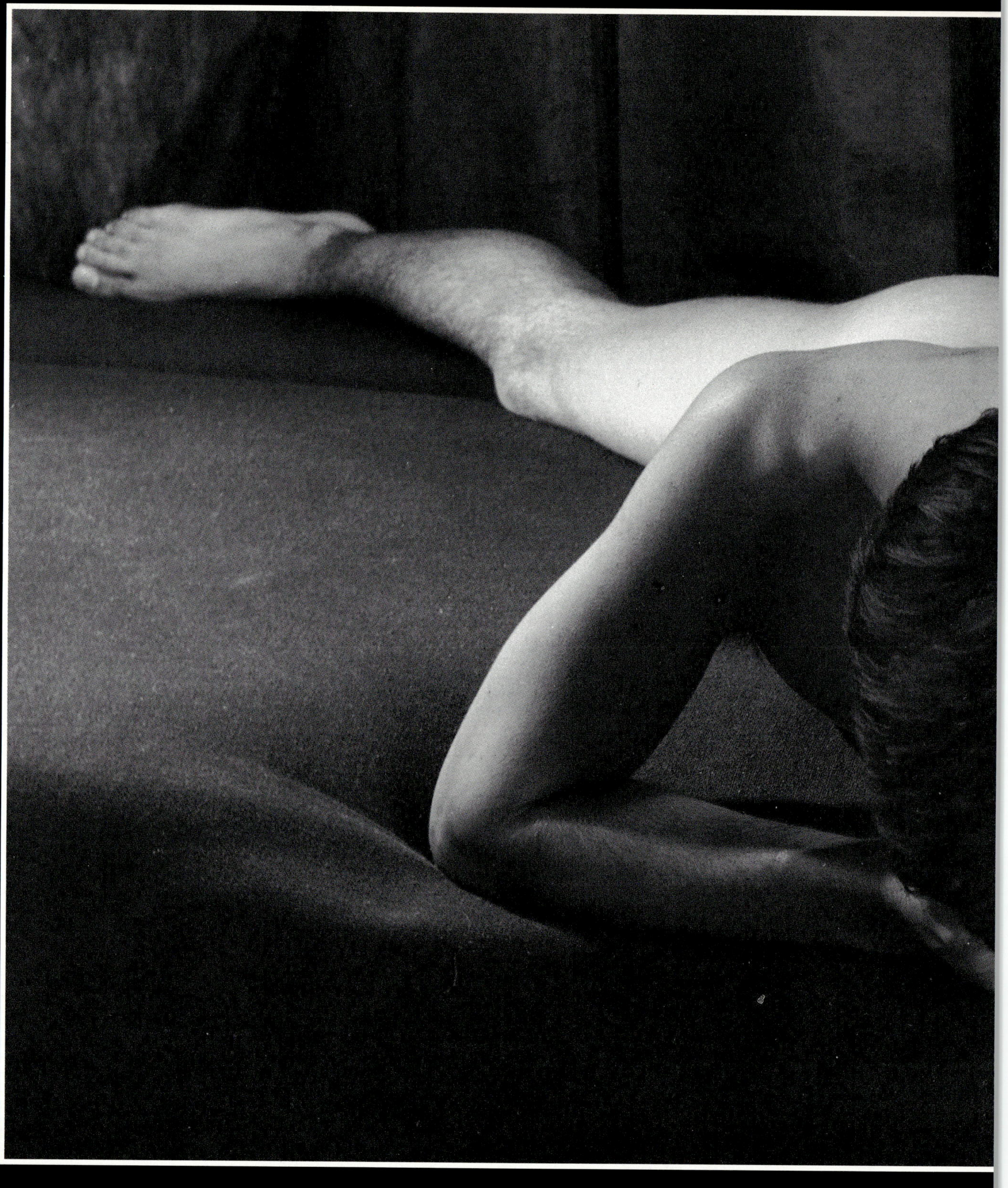

 John

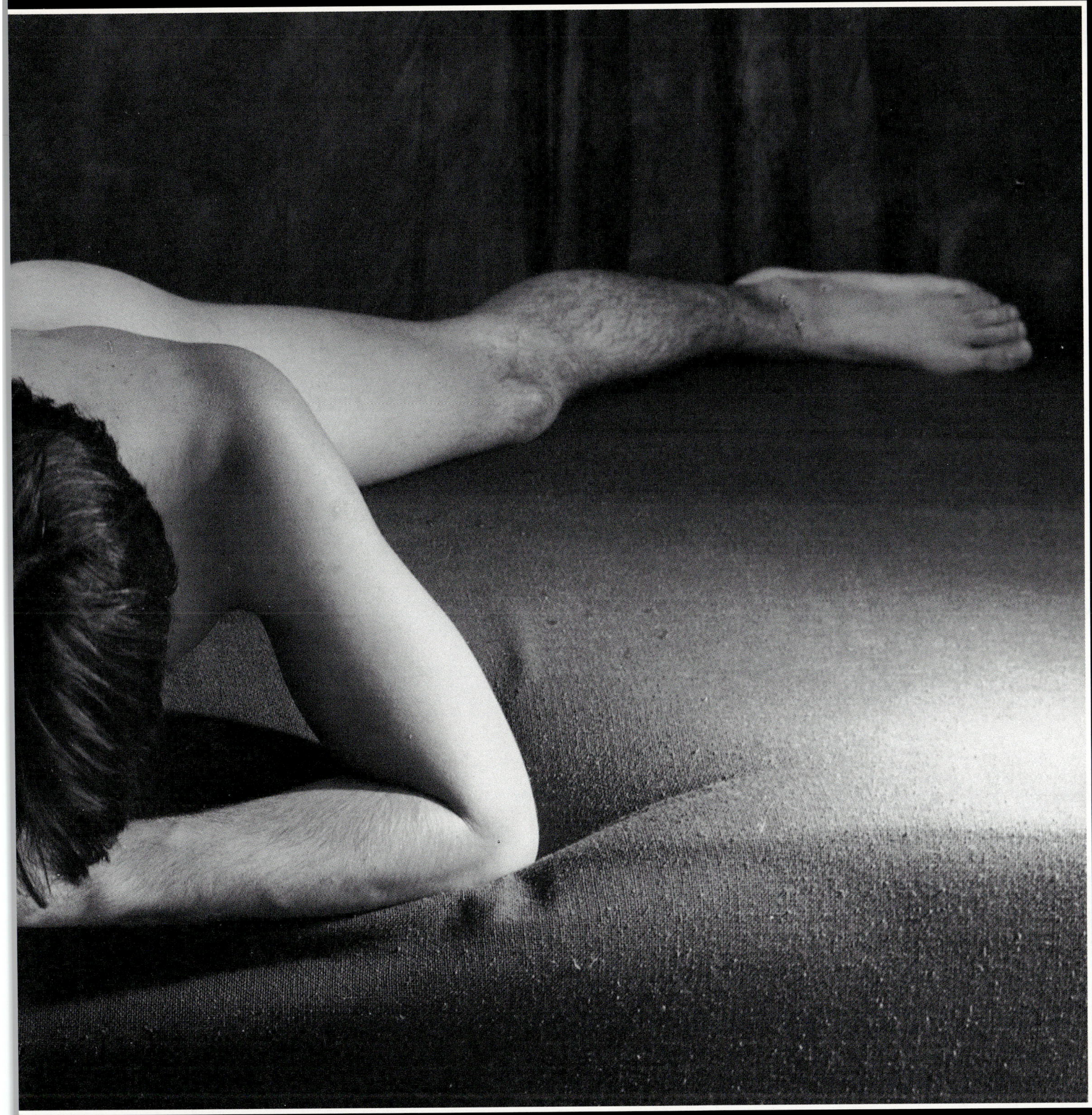

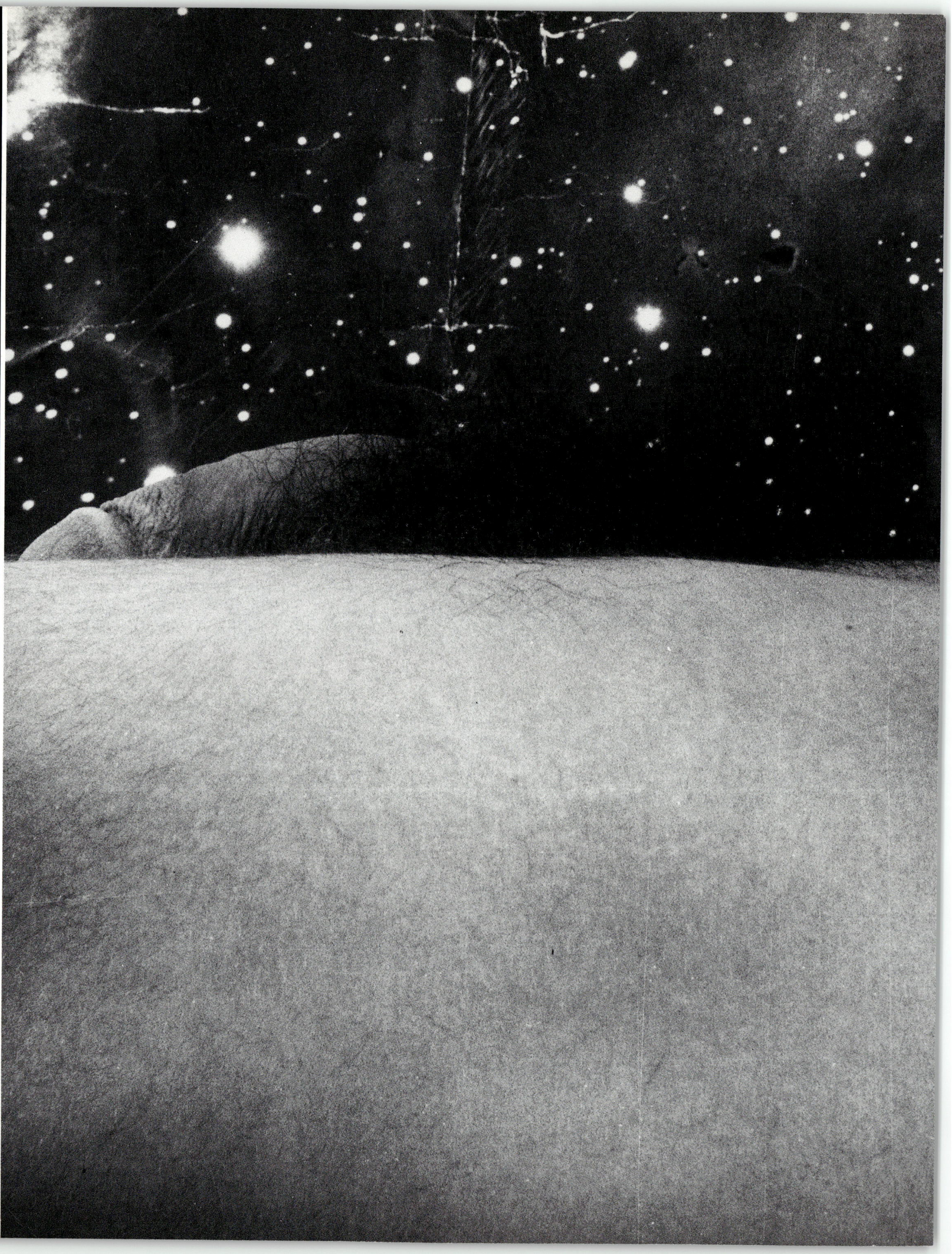

John

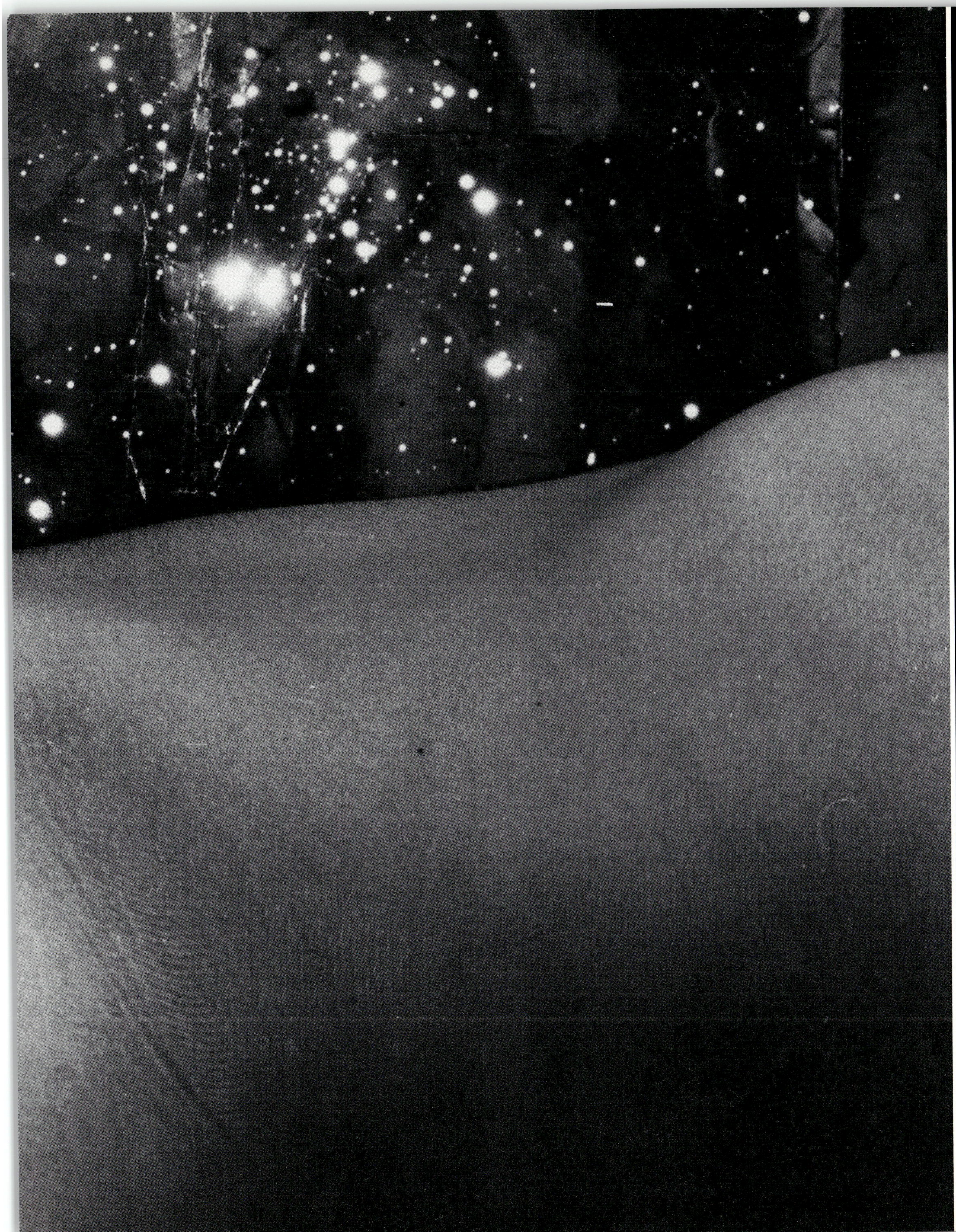

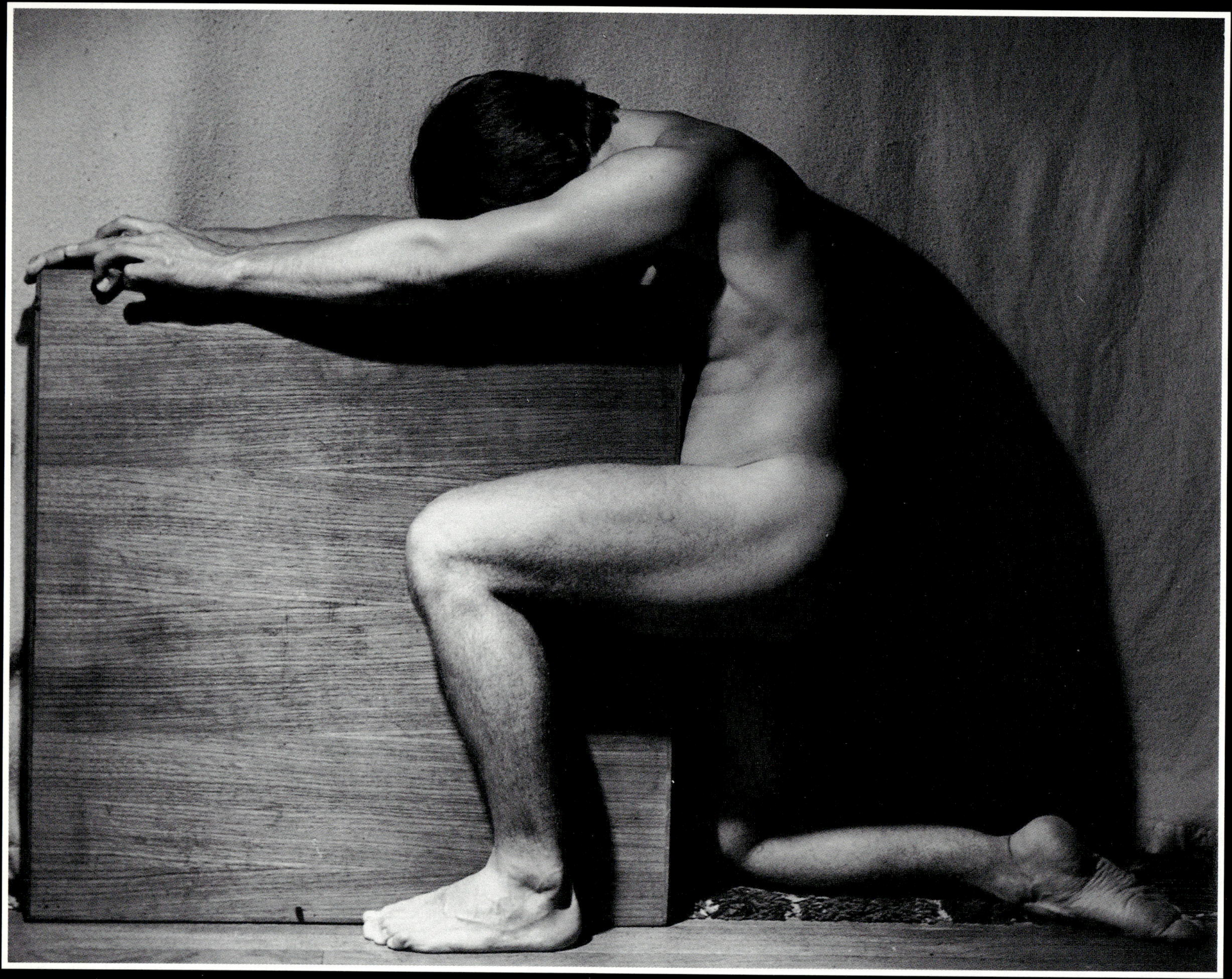

Sean

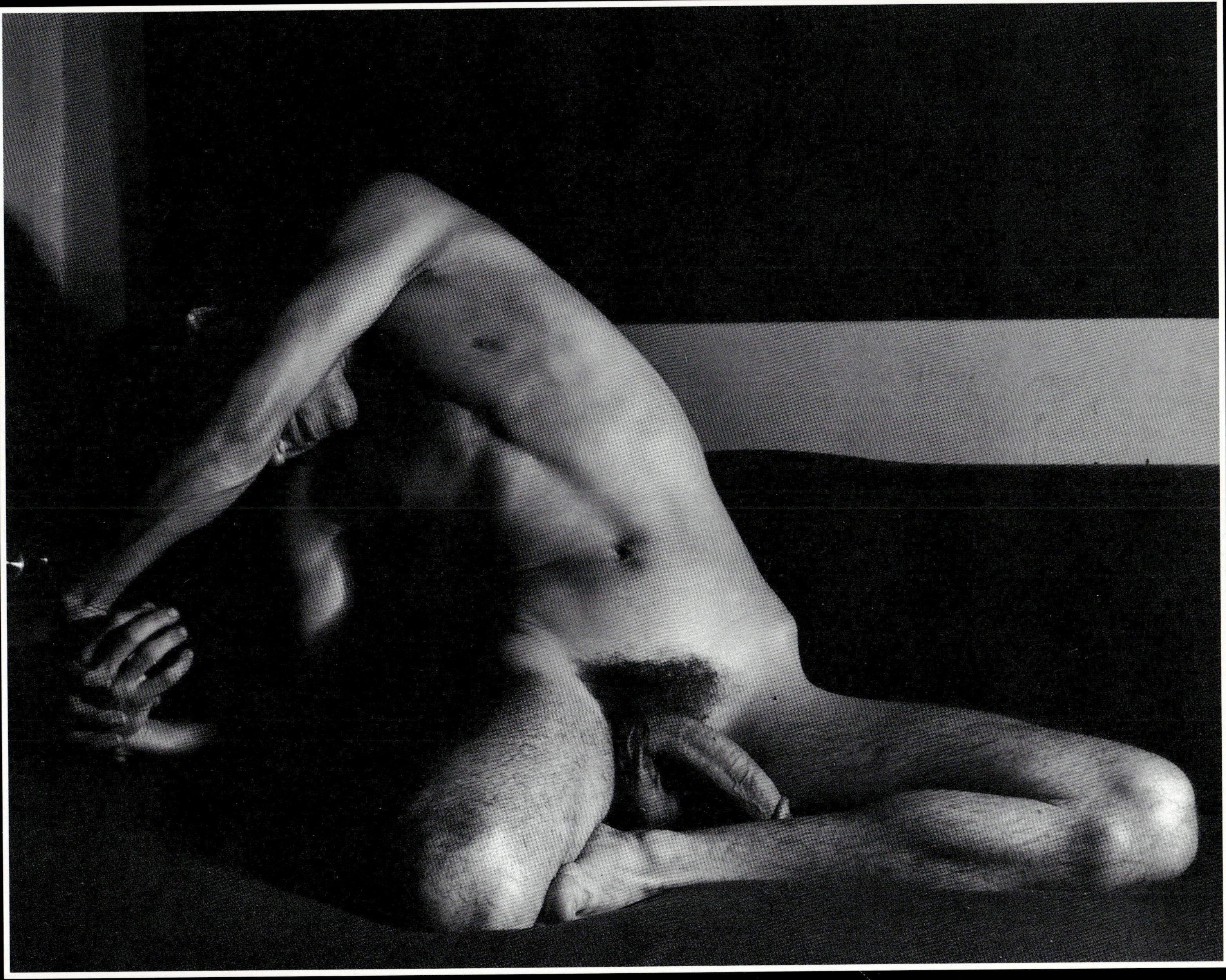

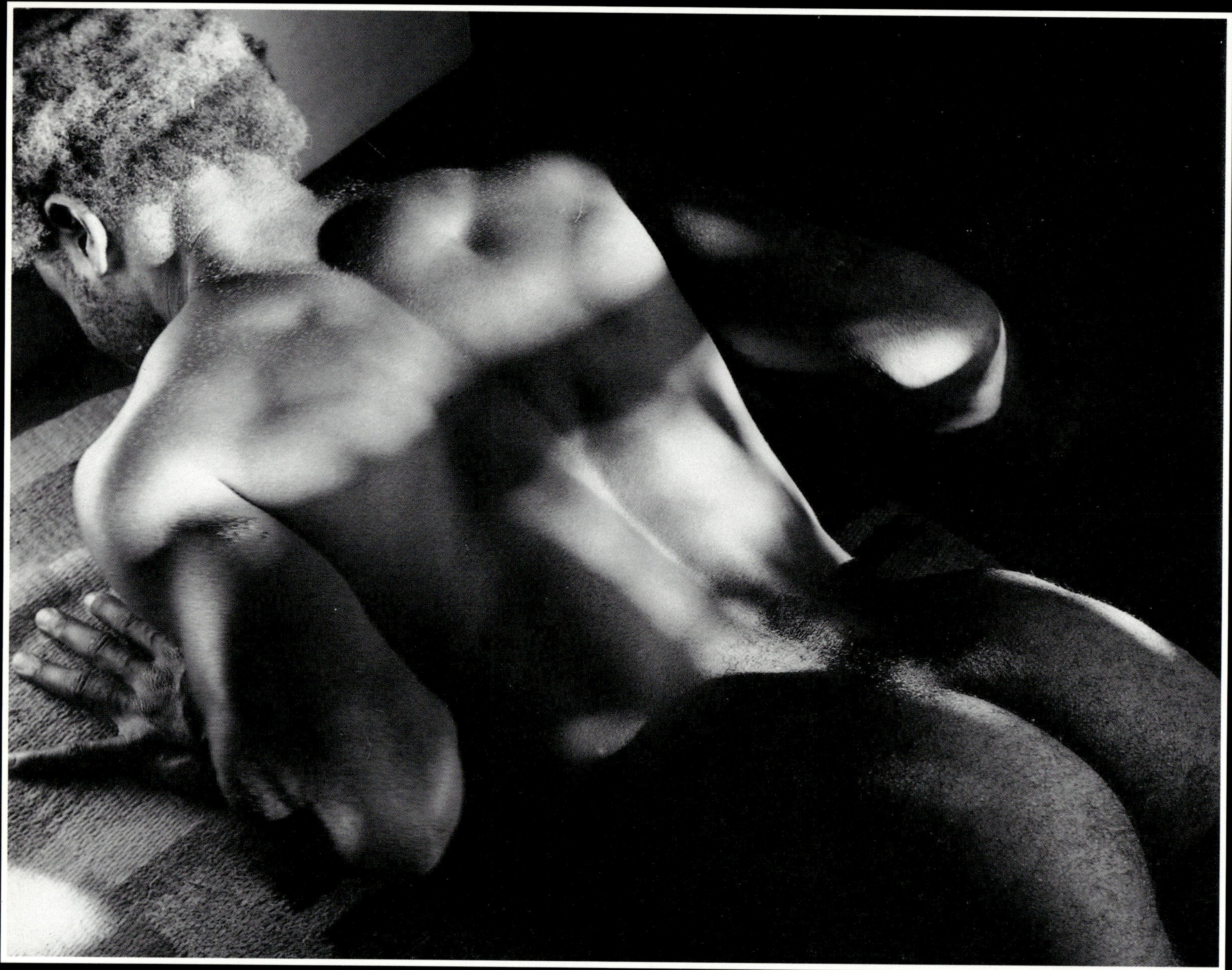

 Robbin

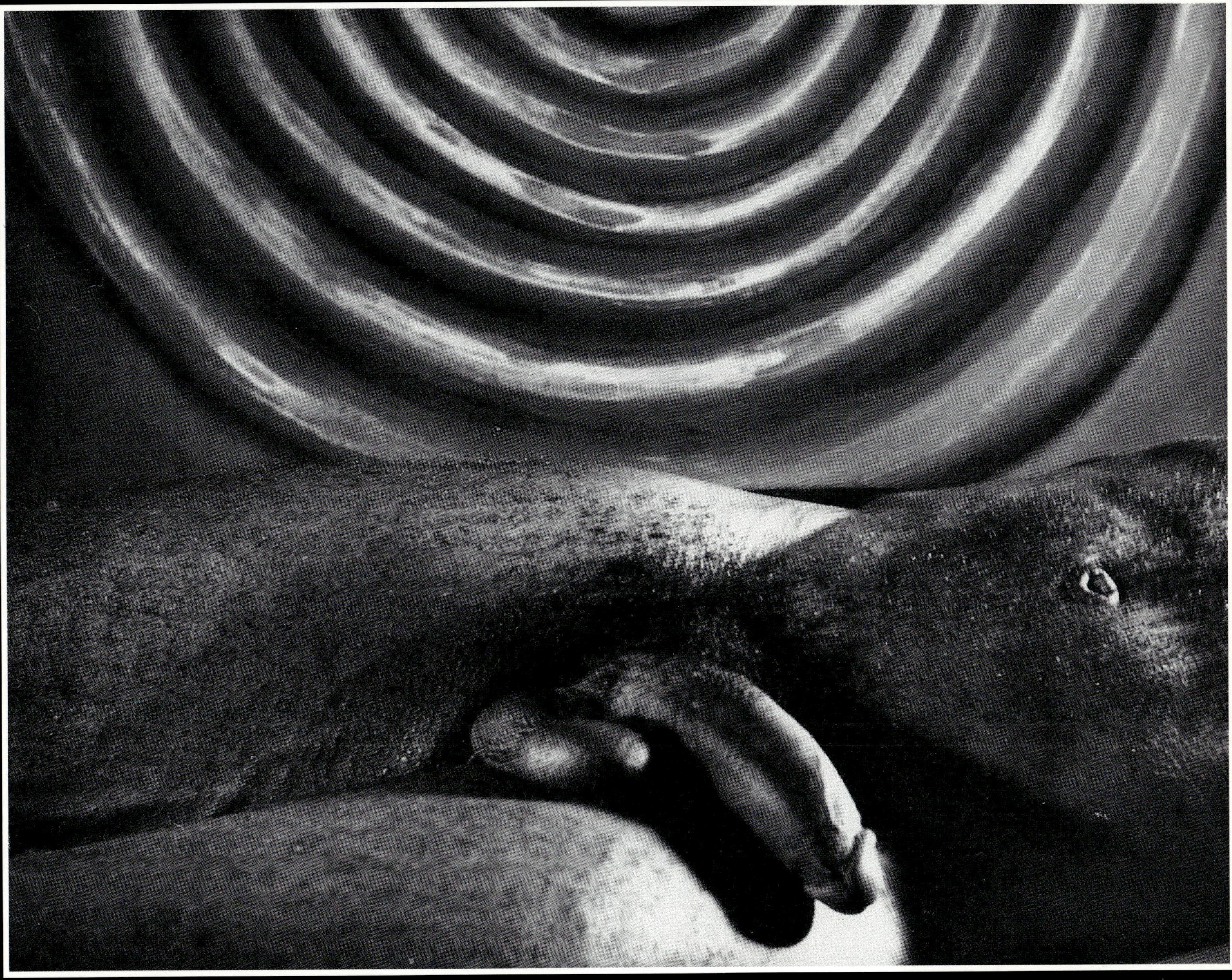

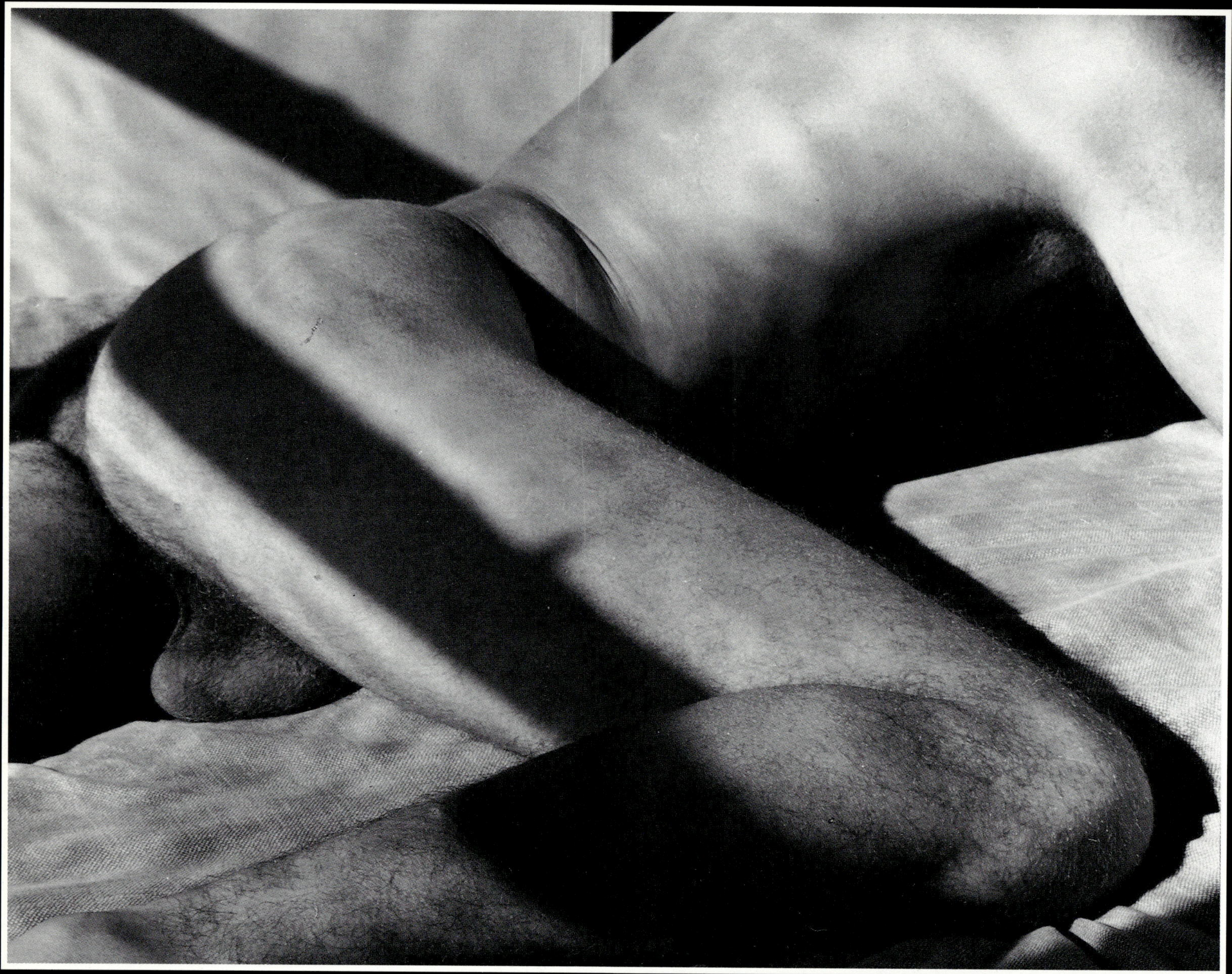

George

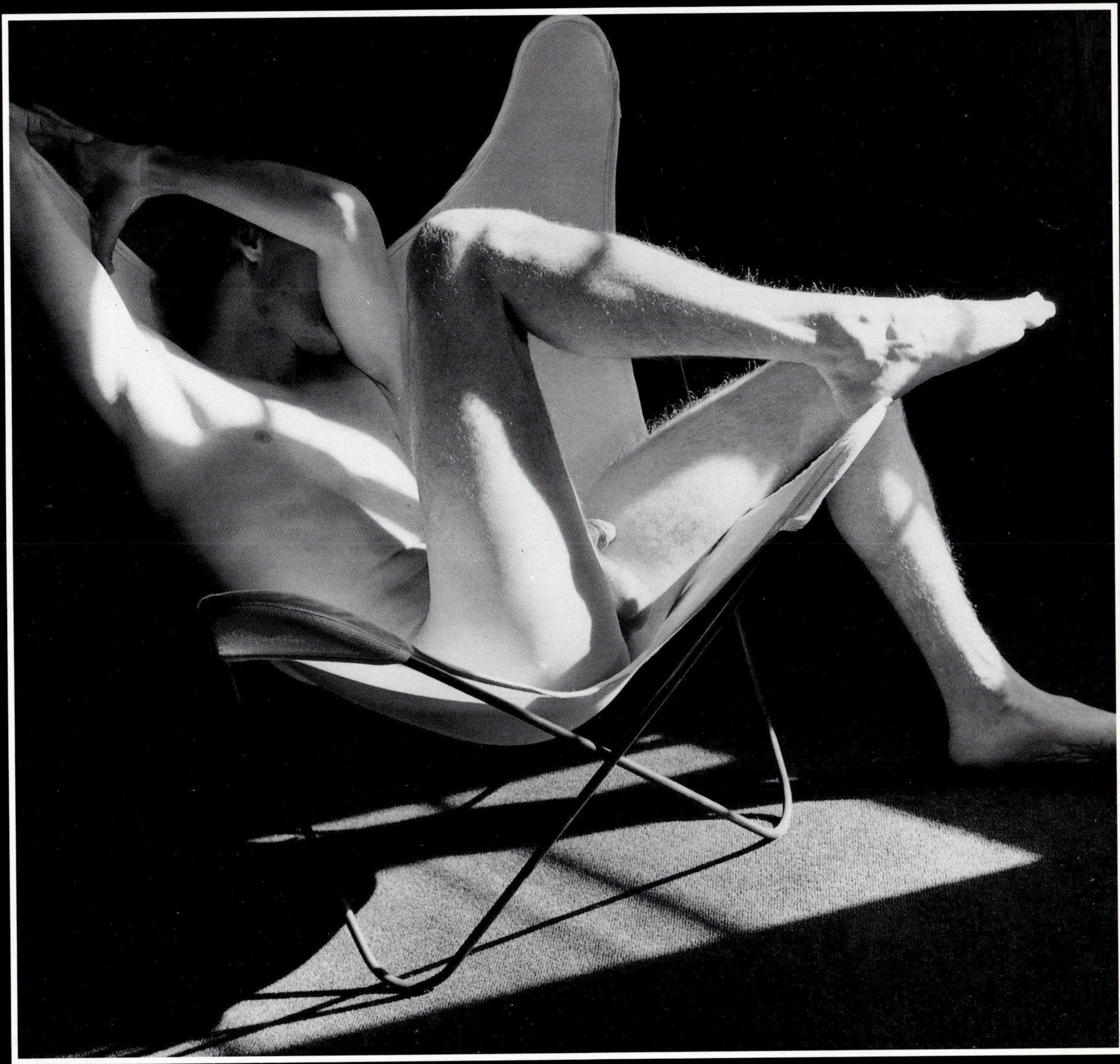

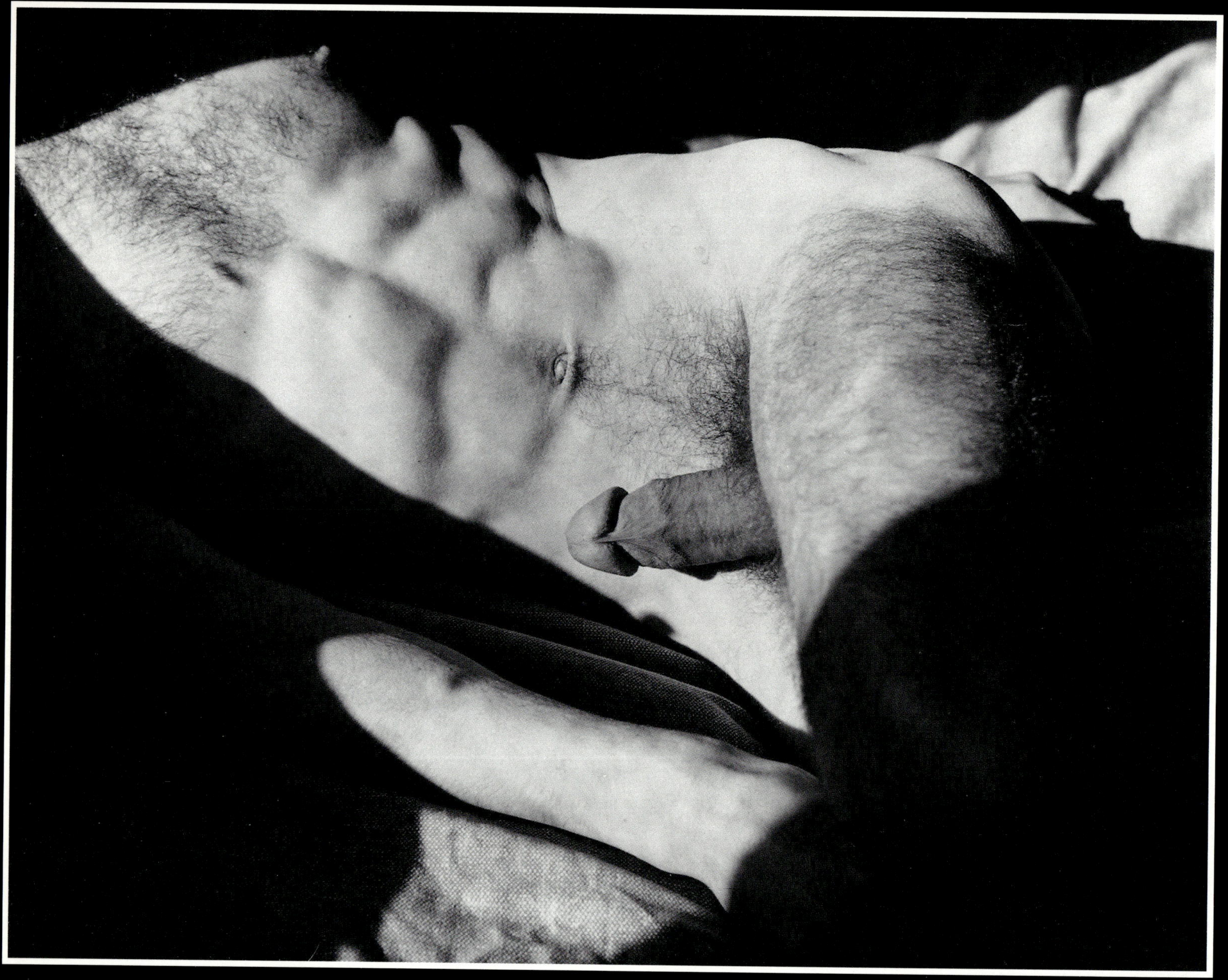

 Mike C

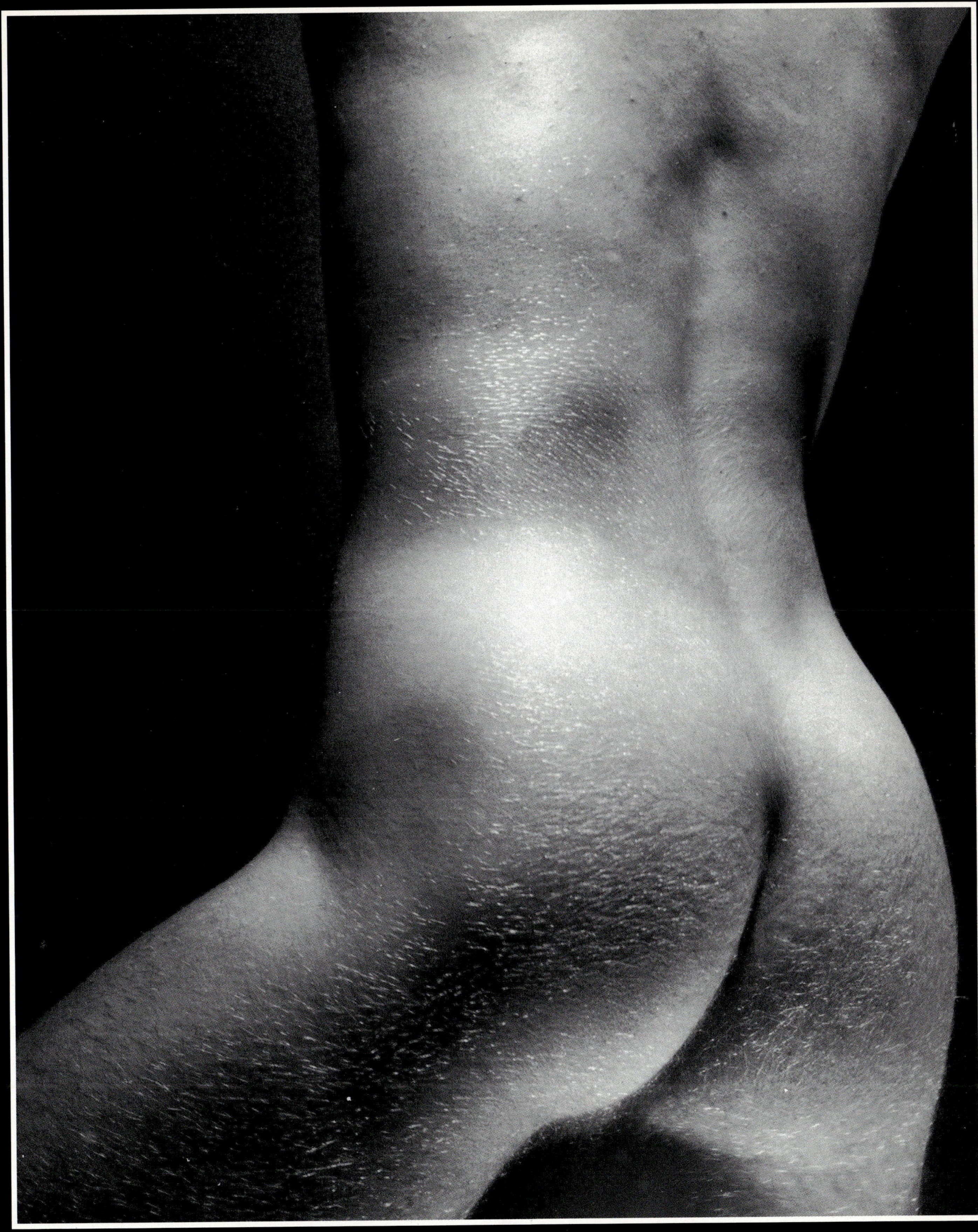

David

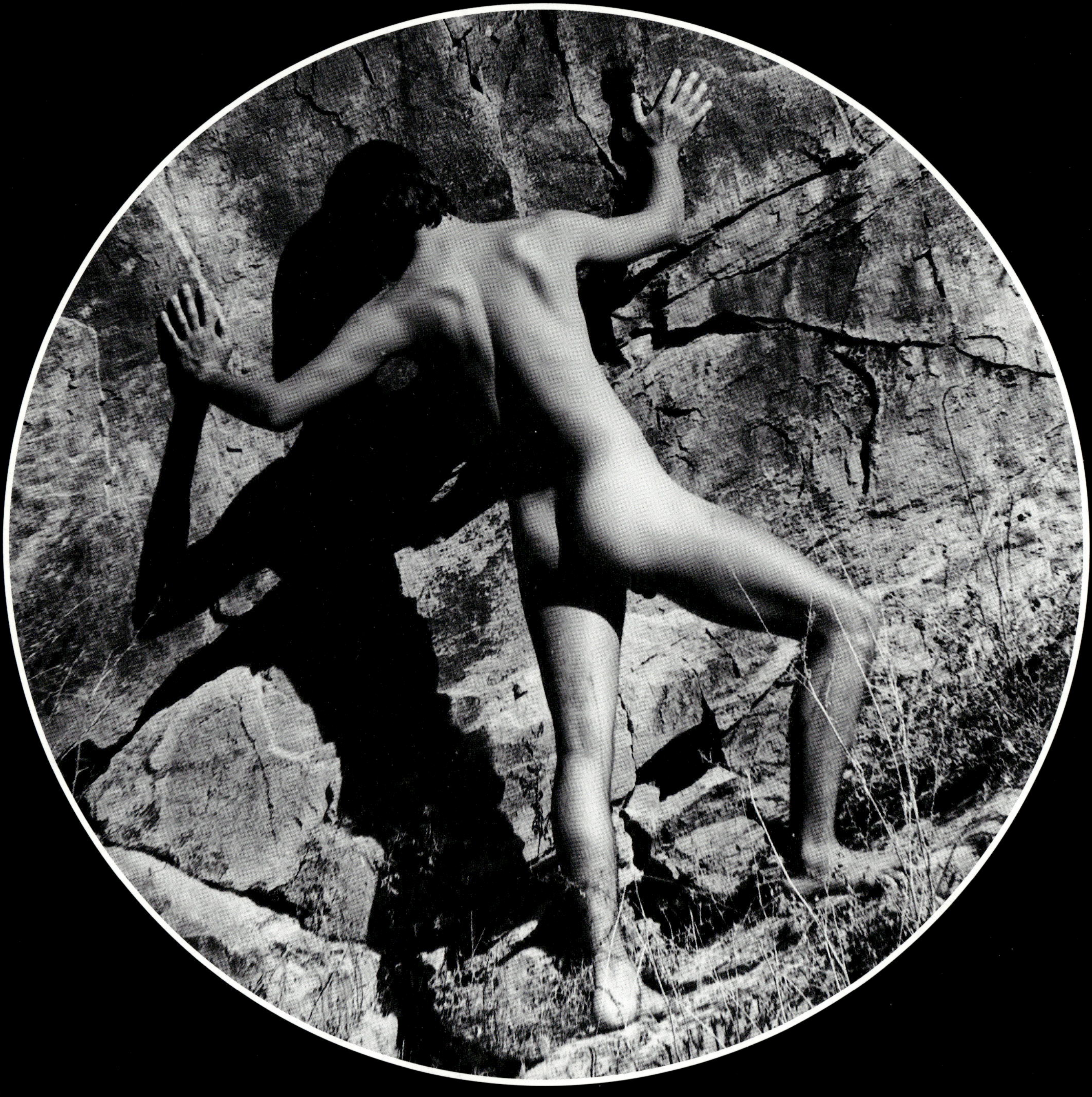

 Michael S

PHOTOGRAPHY
from GMP Publishers Ltd.

These are but two titles from our extensive list of exciting photographic collections.

KOUROS

Photographs by John S Barrington
With an Introduction by Emmanuel Cooper

John S Barrington was at the forefront of post-war male photography in Britain. He has consistently produced work that has challenged the repressive censors of a prudish and homophobic British state.
His photographs combine classical ideals of male beauty with a strong erotic undertone.

60 duotone plates
(256 x 228)mm, 72 pages, £14.95

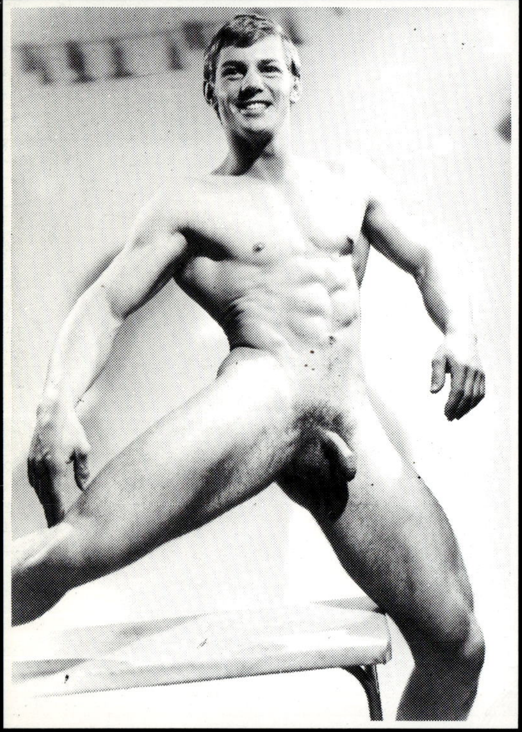

BLACK MALE/WHITE MALE

Photographs by Rotimi Fani-Kayode
With an Introduction by Alex Hirst

These photographs by the late young Nigerian photographer express the belief that magic, masquerade and erotic delirium are essential elements in challenging the impoverishment of the soul. They represent a photographic fusion of Yoruba and Western civilisation.

60 duotone plates
(256 x 228)mm, 72 pages, £12.95

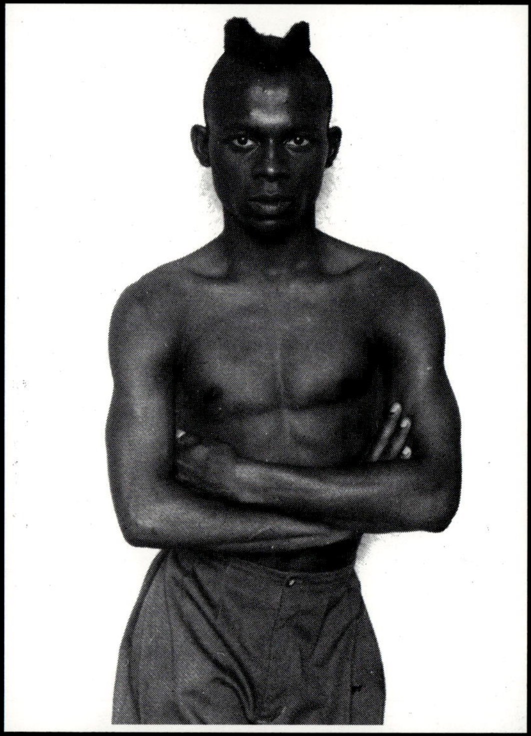